Jew and Non-Jew
Israelites

Those Who Accepted Jesus and Became
Known as Christians, the Prophesied
New Name for God's Covenant People

Thou seest brother, how many thousands of Jews
there are which believe. Acts 21:20

Why, in following the footprints of the first Christians,
do we discover a paradox? Read how the author explains
why millions of descendants of those "thousands of Jews"
assume they are not Israelites! Are you among them?

by Jaye S. Torgerson

Christian Israel Press™ ✝

Copyright © 2013, 2014 by Jaye S. Torgerson

First printing, September 2013
Second printing, February 2014

Jew and Non-Jew Israelites
by Jaye S. Torgerson

Printed in the United States of America

ISBN 978-0-9897947-0-1

Unless otherwise indicated, Bible quotations are taken from the King James Version of the Bible.

Bible quotations marked RSV are taken from the Revised Standard Version of the Bible.

www.christianisraelpress.com

DEDICATION

This book is dedicated to the memory of William Tyndale, the sixteenth-century Protestant reformer who was strangled and burned at the stake for making God's Word, the Bible, available in the common language of his day; and to others like him, the Huguenots and the Waldenses, to all since who were willing to be persecuted, to suffer and die for a truth denied and forbidden by the government and religious establishment in their day. May these martyrs rest in peace as they sleep in Jesus until the end of the age; until they awake on that glorious day when the Lord himself will descend from heaven with a shout and the dead in Christ rise first. Hallelujah, come quickly, Lord Jesus.

TABLE OF CONTENTS

INTRODUCTION

The title of this book does not contain a contradiction of terms known as an oxymoron. It has that appearance, but only if we define these words based upon supposition by hearing them in a modern context. During the Bible narrative there was a distinction between Israel and Judah, and between those of Judah who resided in Judea and those in Galilee. Much confusion has been created by teachers who do not recognize these distinctions while attempting to write and speak regarding the covenant people.

A famous person once said, "If you would speak with me, define your terms." Controversy results when two parties, while in serious conversation, use the same term but in a different sense. Nowhere is this more common than in discussions regarding Scripture. We have Bibles; we read the context wherein its terms are defined, but for some reason we do not always repeat them based upon the same. Or, when we do, they may not be understood by those with whom we are speaking.

In reading *Jew and Non-Jew Israelites,* you will develop a Biblical understanding of key terms such as *Jews* and *Gentiles.* By following these as applied by the Bible writers, you will discover they have primary and secondary definitions. For example, *Jew* in the Old Testament appears mostly in a tribal and national sense. It identifies Israelites in the southern kingdom *(Judah/house of Judah)* as opposed to those in the north.

This explains applications of *Jew* in contradistinction to *Israel*. The Bible writers were comparing Israelites who were called Jews to those who were not. These were the remaining ten tribes in the northern kingdom *(the house of Israel)*—the mysterious "lost tribes of Israel." Distinct and separate from Judah, they were greater in number, but because they play a lesser role in the Bible story are often forgotten.

During a 400-year gap in the Bible narrative, between the prophecy of Malachi and the advent of Christ, is a change in the way *Jew* is applied. In the Old Testament it identified the Judah portion of Israel and now describes the same, but who are geographically divided between Judea and Galilee. Those of Galilee were not, in a geographical sense, Jews (Judeans); they were Jews in a tribal and religious sense only. When John wrote, *Jesus walked in Galilee: for he would not walk in Jewry* (John 7:1), he was describing a Galilean Jew (Jesus) who would not walk in Judea *(Jewry)* because the Jews there (as opposed to Galilee) tried to kill him. Context tells us the Galilean Israelites were not *Jews/Jewry*; they were not of Judea as were the scribes and Pharisees.

And then is *Jew* in a religious sense. When Paul wrote, *For he is not a Jew, which is one outwardly* (Rom. 2:28), he was not telling us that such were not Israelites. He was describing Israelites who were professing Jews only.

These are but a few examples wherein *Jew* is limited to a tribal/national, geographical, or religious sense, which is usually revealed in its context. In cases where it is not, where the context is less than clear, the sense must be determined by seeking information in other applications and/or related subject matter. For this reason, because *Jew* is defined in a variety of ways and in a centuries-old setting, we should not attempt to interpret Scripture based upon a modern and mostly secular application of the word.

Correctly observed, the rules of context will lead to eye-opening discoveries. Chief among these is an error, an error upon which the dominant dispensationalist-futurist method of interpretation is based. Used as an opening line by evangelical leaders, this error is repeated as—"Because Israel rejected Jesus." In reading the scores of Scripture texts quoted in this book you will discover that this statement, only partially true, disagrees with Isaiah's and other prophecies. It cannot be reconciled with Scripture references describing the first Christians as *thousands of Jews.* Neither can it be reconciled with New Covenant congregations, (i.e., the church) which are clearly described as inclusive of Israelites.

Read the evidence in this book and you will no longer accept, without question, a mantra ("Israel rejected Jesus") used as the basis for identifying latter-day Israel. In seeing through this veil, most evangelical Christians will recognize themselves as one of today's millions of descendants of those thousands of Messianic Israelites long ago.

Also based on the mantra of rejection and contradicted by Scripture is that the prophesied *new covenant with the house of Israel and with the house of Judah* (Jer. 31:31) did not work with these people. The author explains how *the epistle to the Hebrews* identifies these Hebrew-Israelites as Christians and how chapters 8-10 describe the prophesied *new covenant* as, not on hold, but in effect two thousand years ago. You will be surprised to learn that the futurist interpretation of Daniel's seventieth-week prophecy, and chapters 4-19 of Revelation, are a recent phenomenon. Discover how they disagree with classical Protestant teaching and were not taught by evangelical greats as recent as Charles H. Spurgeon (1834-1892).

We were told by Jesus to *search the scriptures* (John 5:39). About two thousand years ago a synagogue in a city called

Berea did just that. They searched, whether it was so that Jesus was the Christ; whether it was true that the prophesied Messiah had come in the flesh. As a result many were added to the thousands of Jews who, because they accepted Jesus and the New Covenant, would no longer be known by that name. These were the first Christians, and whose descendants also would be known as Christians by Israel's prophesied *new name* (Isaiah 62:2; 65:15).

Beginning with Peter's vision *(God hath showed me that I should not call any man common or unclean* [Acts 10:28]) in AD 41, the gospel was preached to uncircumcised non-Jew Israelites of the Diaspora. But we assume, because they are called *Gentiles,* they were of non-Israelitish ancestry. Overlooking contextual evidence such as *Abraham our father* (Rom. 4:1), *our father Isaac* (Rom. 9:10), and others, we assume because they were not Jews, they could not be Israelites. Despite evidence to the contrary, we identify these Christians based upon a religious tradition, one which assumes all Israelites were of the tribe and nation of Judah and therefore Jews (i.e., Judahites).

That this is not true is evidenced by the plethora of texts describing Judah in contradistinction to Israel. Overlooking these we then overlook the fact that most of the northern kingdom, i.e., *house of Israel,* did not return to Palestine when deported by the Assyrians seven hundred years before Christ. Divorced by God and scattered among the nations, they, unlike Judah, do not have a prominent role in the Bible narrative. Until reappearing as *Gentiles* in the first century, they are little mentioned. For this reason, because much of the Bible story centers on Jews—on the Judah portion of Israel—we tend to assume all Israelites were Jews. This is not correct.

The reading of the gospels and epistles, before, or without reading the first thirty-nine books, can be a source of confusion. Too often we skip that which contains Israel's history. This has resulted in evangelicals who do not understand the connection between non-Jew Israelites called *the lost sheep of the house of Israel* (Matt. 15:24) and Christians called *Gentiles* in the New Testament epistles. They do not realize that when Jesus walked in Palestine most Israelites *(the twelve tribes which are scattered abroad* [James 1:1]) were in dispersion and had been for centuries.

The Judean Pharisees knew this (*will he go unto the dispersed* [John 7:35]), but for some reason today's religious establishment does not. They would have us focus on the dispersion as occurring when the Romans came against Jerusalem in AD 70. This cannot be reconciled with *twelve tribes which are scattered abroad*, with Israelites already *dispersed*, (and obviously Christian) when James wrote his epistle. Traditionally, James is dated in the middle forties or early sixties, just before his death.

In this book, we will search the Scriptures for *Jews* and *Gentiles* while making a critical analysis of texts containing these words. This will be done with intellectual honesty; we will not read into a text things which are not there. Neither will we cherry-pick verses; we will not use a certain text or texts while ignoring others pertinent to the subject. If a related text appears to disagree, the illusion of contradiction will be explained using proper hermeneutics. The author firmly believes Scripture does not contradict Scripture; interpretations only do that.

Concise and to the point, *Jew and Non-Jew Israelites* does not take long to read. It required much time and research, but not a lengthy book to convey a truth so simple. As we ask the Holy Spirit for discernment, let us begin by examining the distinction between Judah and Israel.

CHAPTER 1

THE DISTINCTION BETWEEN JUDAH AND ISRAEL

Strong's Exhaustive Concordance,[1] which lists each occurrence of every word in the Authorized King James Version, reveals the word Jew as first appearing in 2 Kings, about 1,200 years after the call of Abraham.

> Then Rezin king of Syria and Pekah son of Remaliah king of Israel came up to Jerusalem to war: and they besieged Ahaz, but could not overcome him. At that time Rezin king of Syria recovered Elath to Syria, and drove the Jews from Elath: and the Syrians came to Elath, and dwelt there unto this day. So Ahaz sent messengers to Tiglathpileser king of Assyria, saying, I am thy servant and thy son: come up, and save me out of the hand of the king of Israel, which rise up against me.   2 Kings 16:5-7

The above text describes Pekah, king of Israel, as at war with Ahaz, king of Judah. Rezin, king of Syria, had driven Ahaz and the Jews from Elath, who then sought an alliance with

---

[1] Available online in whole-verse form at *blueletterbible.com*

Assyria in their defense against Israel and Syria. *Israel,* in other words, was warring with—*the Jews.* That the word *Israel* would appear in contradistinction to *the Jews* is confusing if one has been taught to believe all Israelites were Jews. This, obviously, was not the case when the afore-mentioned event occurred (about 740 BC). To understand the origin of Israelites called Jews one must recognize that after the death of King Solomon the twelve tribes became divided into two nations.

In the ninth century BC, ten of the twelve tribes, provoked by oppressive taxation, successfully revolted against Solomon's son, King Rehoboam, in Jerusalem. Jeroboam became their king and Samaria their ruling city (1 Kings 12 and 2 Chron. 10-11). They, as the greater portion of God's covenant people, retained the name Israel while also identi-fied as *house of Israel, children of Israel, Ephraim,* and some-times *Samaria,* after their ruling city. It was the remaining two tribes, Judah and Benjamin, ruled from Jerusalem, who became collectively known as *Judah, house of Judah, chil-dren of Judah, Jerusalem,* and/or for short, *Jews,* a derivative corruption of the term Judahites. Not until this time were any among the twelve tribes called Jews, a term correctly applied to Israelites of Judah only.

Breaking the Covenant

After about two hundred years as a separate nation, the ten-tribed northern kingdom had forsaken the Law of the Lord (YHWH),[2] thus breaking its covenant with Yahweh, their God, and was coming under judgment.

> Therefore the Lord was very angry with Israel, and
> removed them out of his sight: there was none left

---

[2] The Tetragrammaton; the four Hebrew characters that represent the personal name of the God of the Bible. Rendered LORD or GOD in English translations, it is probably best pronounced as *Yahweh.*

but the tribe of Judah only.... So was Israel carried away out of their own land to Assyria unto this day.

2 Kings 17:18; 23

In a series of deportations lasting from 745 BC to 721 BC, most of ten-tribed Israel was driven from the old Promised Land never to return. About 130 years later, Judah also was in wholesale disobedience and coming under judgment:

> And the Lord said, I will remove Judah also out of my sight, as I have removed Israel,.... And it came to pass... that Nebuchadnezzar king of Babylon came...against Jerusalem.... And the city was broken up.... And the king of Babylon smote them, and slew them.... So Judah was carried away out of their land.
>
> 2 Kings 23:27; 25:1, 4, 21

An exhaustive study of Scripture on this subject will reveal that most of Judah, like most of Israel a century earlier, was deported to Assyria and would not return to Palestine. This was in fulfillment of warnings by God centuries earlier that, if they abandoned the Law of the Lord the covenant made on Mount Sinai:

- I will scatter you among the heathen (Lev. 26:33).
- I will scatter you abroad among the nations (Neh. 1:8).

Thus began the Diaspora, the dispersion of Israel and Judah. This occurred hundreds of years before the Roman army came against Jerusalem in AD 70.

A Remnant of Judah Returns

Judah, unlike Israel (Jer. 3:8), was not given a bill of divorcement. Neither would all Judahites remain in exile. After seventy years of captivity in Babylon a *remnant* (Ezra 3:8; 9:8) would return to Jerusalem. In chapter 2 of Ezra and chapter 7 of Nehemiah, this remnant, this portion only of Judah, is recorded as *forty and two thousand three hundred and three score.* They are reckoned by genealogy and called *Jews* (Neh. 1:2) because they were, primarily, of the Judah nation. It was they to whom *were committed the oracles of God* (Rom. 3:2), and who were to administer the kingdom of God, a responsibility that would be taken from them centuries later (Matt. 21:43). It was they, this remnant of Judah, who would rebuild the temple and grow into the community of Israelites which occupied Palestine at the coming of Jesus the Messiah. In the meantime, those who remained in exile, those who did and would not return were becoming:

- The dispersed among the Gentiles (John 7:35).
- Other sheep I have which are not of this fold (John 10:16).
- The children of God that were scattered abroad (John 11:52).
- The strangers scattered throughout Pontus, Galatia, Cappadocia, Asia and Bithynia (1 Peter 1:1).
- The twelve tribes which are scattered abroad (James 1:1).

To ignore, then, the distinction between Judah and Israel while calling all Israelites *Jews* is not in accordance with historical facts regarding the Covenant People.

Eighth Century BC Judah and Israel

CHAPTER 2

FROM JUDAHITES TO JUDEANS

When reading the New Testament it is important to remember that most of twelve-tribed Israel at that time was outside of Palestine and had been for hundreds of years. Also important to recognize is that first-century Palestinian Israelites were comprised mostly of Judah and were concentrated in two geographical areas, Judea and Galilee.

In the rear of most Bibles are maps. One of these will show Palestine, in New Testament times, with Judea and Galilee separated by Samaria. For this reason *Jew*, in the New Testament, is often used, in a geographical sense only, to distinguish between Judahites in Judea and those in Galilee. What follows is an explanation of applications wherein the context of *Jew* identifies Judahites of Judea only.

> After these things Jesus walked in Galilee for he would not walk in Jewry (Judea) because the Jews (Judeans) sought to kill him.
>
> John 7:1 (parentheses mine)

The reason as to why Jesus walked in Galilee rather than Judea is meaningless if, as implied by most teachers, the

Galileans also were Jews (Judeans). They were not. They were Israelites, but they were not of Judea and therefore were not Jews as Jews are defined in the context of John 7:1. One does not have to be a dictionary editor to recognize that words can have secondary definitions; *Jew* is no exception to this.

Jesus was of Nazareth, which was located in Galilee. Also of Galilee were eleven of his twelve disciples. Coincidence or not, Judas Iscariot, because he was of Kerioth in Judea, was the only Judean among them. Some time later Jesus was back in Judea *(Jewry)* when:

> The Jews (Judeans) took up stones again to stone him…. but he escaped out of their hand, And went away again beyond Jordan…. And many believed on him there…. Then after that saith he to his disciples, let us go into Judea again. His disciples say unto him, Master, the Jews (Judeans) of late sought to stone thee; and goest thou thither again?
> John 10:31, 39, 40, 42, 11:7-8 (parentheses mine)

It was the religious authorities in Judea—the scribes, Pharisees, chief priests, Sadducees, and elders of the people—who rejected and persecuted Jesus (Mark 8:31; Luke 9:22). They were called Jews, in contradistinction to Israelites in Galilee, because Judea is where they lived. This is not someone's opinion; it is the defining of a word based upon context. Context and it alone should be the primary determining factor, the final arbitrator when deciding which sense the Bible writers intended for *Jew* to be understood.

Again, it was the religious authorities in Judea, collectively referred to as *the Jews,* who rejected Jesus, *the common people heard him gladly* (Mark 12:37); *the Galileans received him* (John 4:45). It was the common Israelite, in Judea and from Galilee who, when Jesus was coming into Jerusalem:

> Took branches of palm trees, and went forth to meet
> him, and cried, Hosanna, blessed is the king of Israel
> that cometh in the name of the Lord.   John 12:13

It was the Judean Pharisees who, when seeing *the common people,* the masses of Israelites, accepting Jesus, *said among themselves, perceive ye how ye prevail nothing? Behold, the world is gone after him* (John 12:13, 19). The gospels are replete with references to *the multitudes* of Israelites, *the common people* in Judea and Galilee accepting Jesus—as a minority among them, mostly in Judea *(the Jews),* rejected him. When Israel's Messiah appeared in public he is described as surrounded and supported by multitudes of Israelites, by *innumerable multitudes of people* (Luke 12:1, etc.). Had this not been so the Judean scribes and Pharisees, etc., *(the Jews),* would not have perceived him as a threat to their authority and would not have:

> Assembled together...and consulted that they might
> take Jesus by subtilty and kill him.   Matthew 26:4

Contrary then to applications of this word by seminary and Bible college professors, all first-century Palestinian Israelites were not, in a geographical sense, Jews; they were not all of Judea. Neither, when Jesus walked in Palestine, was there a rejection of him by all or most Israelites. It was mostly those in positions of authority and, because they were corrupt, who rejected and persecuted Jesus. They were disproportionately located in Judea, but were not representative of all Judeans, much less Israelites in Galilee and elsewhere.

Also taught by Bible college and seminary professors, and in the spirit of political correctness, is that it was the Romans who killed Jesus. For whose benefit are they willing to ignore and blatantly deny that which was clearly stated by the apostle Paul?

The Jews: Who both killed the Lord Jesus, and their own prophets, and have persecuted us; and they please not God, and are contrary to all men.

1 Thessalonians 2:14-15

This was not condemning of all Israelites in Judea. It was specific of the religious and other authorities—those who killed Jesus and were persecuting the disciples for teaching in his name. Many of the common people and even a few among the Pharisees (Nicodemus, etc.) accepted Israel's Messiah. Not all Judeans were anti-Christ.

> Jesus and other Galileans were not, in a geographical sense, Jews.

These and other applications demonstrate the importance of using context and it alone as the final arbitrator when deciding which meaning the Bible writers intended in using a particular word. One must then ask why the religious establishment ignores the difference between primary and secondary definitions of *Jew*. Why is it not recognized that Jesus and other Galileans were not, in a geographical sense, Jews?

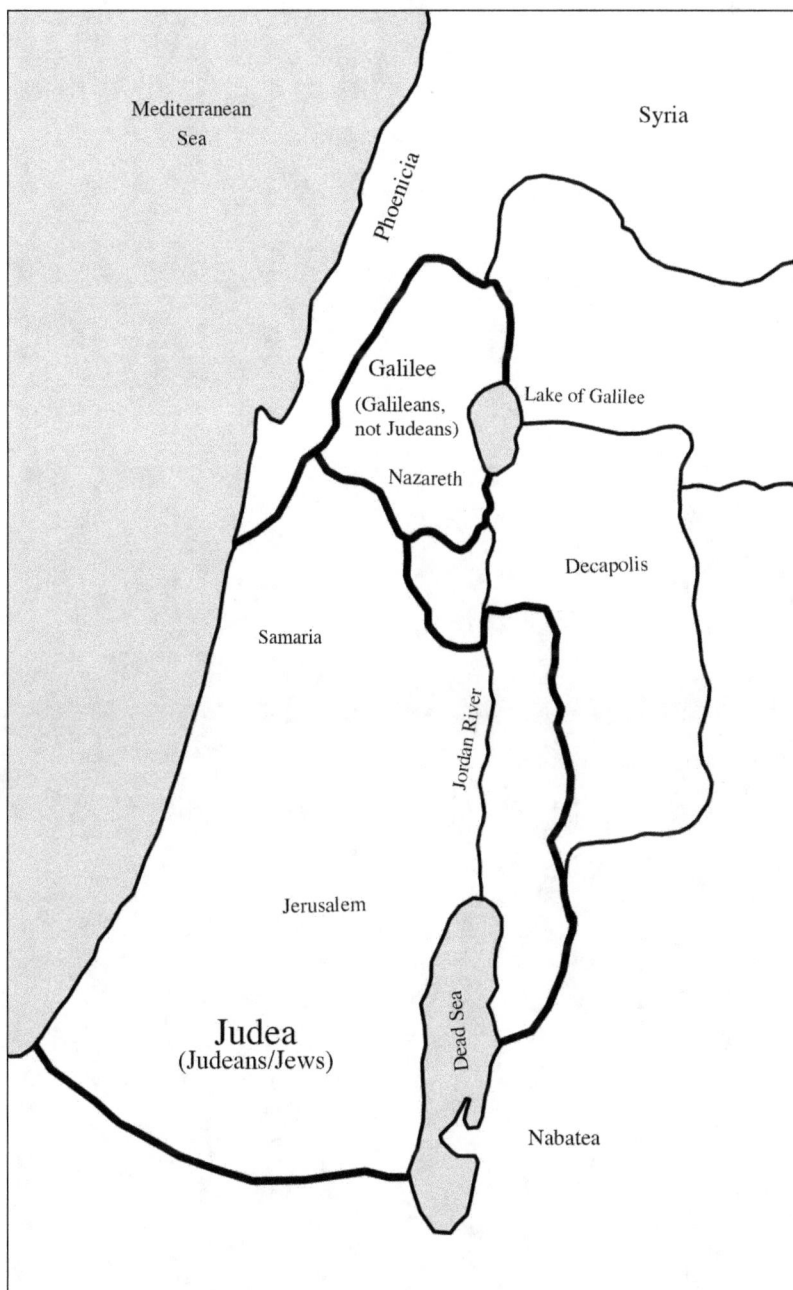

Mediterranean
Sea

Syria

Phoenicia

Galilee
(Galileans,
not Judeans)

Lake of Galilee

Nazareth

Decapolis

Samaria

Jordan River

Jerusalem

Dead Sea

Judea
(Judeans/Jews)

Nabatea

First Century Judea and Galilee

CHAPTER 3

JEW, IN A RELIGIOUS SENSE

From the beginning Israel's religious capital was located in what would later become the nation of Judah. Even so it was not until after the ten-tribed *house of Israel* was divorced by God and driven from the old Promised Land that *Jew* appears in a context describing the religion given by Yahweh God to Israel. The following are examples of this word in that context, one which is not tribal, nor geographical, but religious in meaning.

> Behold, thou art called a Jew..., but if thou be a breaker of the law, thy circumcision is made uncircumcision.... *For he is not a Jew*, which is one outwardly; neither is that circumcision which is outward in the flesh. *But he is a Jew*, which is one inwardly, and circumcision is that of the heart, in the spirit, and not in the letter; whose praise is not of men, but of God.
> Romans 2:17, 25, 28-29 (emphasis mine)

Jew, in a religious context, identified Israelites in and outside of Judea *(Jewry)* who belonged to synagogues affiliated with the temple in Jerusalem. When Paul wrote, *he is not a Jew which is one outwardly,* he was not telling us that those so described were not descended from Jacob-Israel, or that they were not of Judea. He was describing Israelites who, because they were circumcised in the flesh only, were professing Jews only. They were not circumcised in heart; their religion was not in the heart nor in the spirit, but in the letter only. Most of the scribes, Pharisees, and others in authority, especially those in Judea, were in this category and worse. That they were not real, but professing Jews only is demonstrated by the following words of Jesus:

- For had ye believed Moses, ye would have believed me: for he wrote of me. But if ye believe not his writings how shall ye believe my words? (John 5:46-47).
- Why go ye about to kill me? (John 7:19).
- Ye are of your father the devil and the lusts of your father ye will do.... ye are not of God (John 8:44-47).
- He that hateth me hateth my father also....now have they both seen and hated both me and my father (John 15:23-24).

> Jesus, unlike those who opposed him, was—a real Jew.

When the Samaritan woman at the well (John 4:9) called Jesus *a Jew* it was in a religious sense. When Jesus told her, *salvation is of the Jews* (v. 22) it was in the same. He was not giving credibility to the Judean scribes and Pharisees, those who were of their father, the devil, but were called Jews because they lived in Judea. Jesus, when using this word in conversation with the woman, was describing a religion in which one qualified as a real Jew by being circumcised, as Paul stated in Romans 2:29, *in the heart, in the spirit, and not in the letter* only. In this sense Jesus, unlike those who opposed him, was—a real Jew.

The Samaritan woman, like Jesus, was descended from *our father Jacob* (v. 12) and therefore an Israelite (v. 20), but she, unlike Jesus, was not a Jew by religion. She and other non-Judah Israelites, because they were not affiliated with the temple in Jerusalem, were considered as unclean by the Judah portion of Israel, especially those in Judea. This woman was an Israelite, but she was not a Jew, not in a religious, tribal, or in a geographical sense.

Not in the New Testament, but also confusing for most is the use of this word in chapter 8 of Zechariah:

> In those days it shall come to pass, that ten men shall take hold out of all languages of the nations, even shall take hold of the skirt of him that is a Jew, saying, We will go with you: for we have heard that God is with you.   Zechariah 8:23

It is beyond the scope of this writing to explain the entirety of Zechariah's prophecy. Knowing that not all who say they are Jews are, in a religious sense, real Jews, it is reasonable to believe there are limitations on his application of this word. We should not assume that any and all who claim, in a religious or other sense, to meet the qualifications of *him that is a Jew* do so.

The Synagogue of Satan

Corroborating with this word in its religious sense are the last applications of *Jew* in Scripture. These were used by our Lord himself in messages to the churches at Smyrna and Philadelphia. To the Messianic congregation at Smyrna was written:

> I know thy works, and tribulation, and poverty, (but thou art rich) and I know the blasphemy of them which say they are Jews, and are not, but are of the synagogue of Satan.   Revelation 2:9

Again is *Jew* in a religious-only sense. Christ was not telling the church at Smyrna that certain people were not descended from the Judah portion of Israel. He was describing professing-only Jews among Israelites. Being blasphemers they could not have been circumcised in the heart and therefore, unlike Messianic Israelites—were not real Jews. Their attitude was similar, if not identical to the professing-only Jews in Antioch, those who *spake against those things which were spoken by Paul, contradicting and blaspheming* (Acts 13:45).

In reading Paul's epistles you will notice there were Jews and synagogues in countries outside of Palestine. Some of these Diaspora Jews, like those in Antioch, were hostile to the gospel; others were very receptive. When Paul and Silas traveled to Berea in Macedonia and visited a *synagogue of the Jews* (Acts 17:10) we are told that:

> These (Jews) were more noble than those in Thessalonica, in that they received the word with all readiness of mind, and searched the scriptures daily, whether those things were so. Therefore many of them believed.   vv. 11-12 (parenthesis mine)

Prior to Berea, Paul and Silas had preached the gospel to a synagogue of Jews in Thessalonica, where *some of them believed, and consorted with Paul and Silas...But the Jews which believed not, moved with envy, took unto them certain lewd fellows of the baser sort, and gathered a company, and set all the city on an uproar, and assaulted the house of Jason* (Acts 17:4-5).

Throughout the book of Acts the reader finds that Israelites called Jews are described in both a negative and a positive context. On the negative side were non-Messianic Jews, those who denied that Jesus was the Christ. It was they, as will be explained later, who retained the name *Jew*. On the positive side were Messianic Jews, those becoming known as Christians.

The last application of this word in Scripture is our Lord's message to the church at Philadelphia. He assured them:

> Behold, I will make them of the synagogue of Satan,
> which say they are Jews and are not, but do lie;
> behold, I will make them to come and worship before
> thy feet, and to know that I have loved thee.
>
> Revelation 3:9

Here is a second witness, by our Lord himself, to the existence of those who say they are Jews and are not, but are of the synagogue of Satan. Again, this had nothing to do with ancestry. Were this the case he probably would have said something like, "but are of the house of Esau," or, "but are of their father Ishmael," or something else relating to ancestry. Jesus identified these people as of *the synagogue of Satan* for the same reason he told the Judean scribes and Pharisees, *ye are of your father the devil... ye are not of God* (John 8:44, 47). It was not their ancestry, but their theology which condemned them; they were anti-Christ.

Once aware of Revelation 2:9 and 3:9 you will notice how most Judeo-Christian teachers are loath to admit that there were, and might therefore still be, those who say they are Jews and are not, but are of the synagogue of Satan.

Among the reference books in this writer's library is the title, *Liberty Commentary on The New Testament,* published by Liberty Press of Lynchburg, Virginia. Named among its list of contributors are such notables as the late Dr. Jerry Falwell and a dozen or more current and past professors at prominent schools such as Dallas Theological Seminary and Moody Bible Institute. Listed as general editor of the Revelation portion is the well-known Dr. Woodrow M. Kroll who, at that time, was Professor of Religion at Liberty Baptist College.

In fifty-eight pages of commentary Dr. Kroll chooses to not mention *them which say they are Jews, and are not, but are of the synagogue of Satan.* Neither, of course, do he and his fellow dispensationalists acknowledge that there might be among us today, *them which say they are Jews, and are not, but are of the synagogue of Satan.* They would rather, it seems, be caught drunk at the Southern Baptist Convention than acknowledge a past or present synagogue of Satan. Is it not, then, for fear of this element that many Judeo-Christian teachers give Revelation 2:9 and 3:9 the silent treatment? This would be reasonable to assume.

Professing Jews Only

What follows is a partial list of reasons as to why the Judean scribes, Pharisees, and certain other Israelites were not real, but professing Jews only:

- They were, according to Jesus, *hypocrites* (Matthew 15:7; 23:13; 15, etc.).
- They condoned usury by allowing *moneychangers* and other thieves among them to operate in the temple (Mark 11:15; John 2:14-15).
- They, according to Jesus, laid aside *the commandment of God* for *the tradition of men* (Mark 7:1-13).
- They, when told by Jesus, *ye are not of my sheep... took up stones again to stone him* (John 10:26-31).
- They, in a spiritual sense, were not *Abraham's children.* Neither, in the same sense was God their father. Their spiritual father was, according to Jesus, *the devil* (John 8:39-44).
- They, when Lazarus was raised from the dead, began plotting to kill Jesus because real Jews, seeing this miracle, *believed on him* (John 11:43-45).
- They, *consulted that they might put Lazarus also to death; Because that by reason of him many of the Jews* (real Jews)*..., believed on Jesus* (John 12:9-11 [parenthesis mine]).
- They, and *for fear of* them, were the reason real Jews dared not speak openly of Jesus (John 7:13).

- They, and *for fear of* them, were the reason a real Jew, Joseph of Arimathaea, *was a disciple of Jesus, but secretly* (John 19:38).
- They, when crowds of Israelites, when *much people...cried Hosanna; Blessed is the King of Israel that cometh in the name of the Lord* (John 12:13), then plotted to kill, and were successful in murdering Jesus—a real Jew.

CHAPTER 4

A NEW NAME FOR ISRAEL'S RELIGION

Prior to the disciples and other Israelites being *called Christians first in Antioch* (Acts 11:26), the name of Israel's religion was *Jew*. Proselytes also to Judah's religion became known as Jews. Most, if not all of these, would have been in the category of *stranger*, a term often applied to other Hebrew people who, because they were probably born outside of Judah, or for some other reason were not circumcised and therefore were not in the temple genealogical registry in Jerusalem. It was, however, in God's plan that the term *Jew* for those of Israel's religion was temporary only, to be replaced with a new name.

> And thou shalt be called by *a new name*, which the mouth of the Lord shall name.... for the Lord God shall slay thee, and call his servants by *another name*.
> Isaiah 62:2; 65:15 (emphasis mine)

This new name for God's Israel covenant people would be *Christian,* a title first applied in Antioch about AD 41. Those whom God would *slay* during this transition from the name *Jew* to *Christian* were the anti-Christ element headquartered in Jerusalem and Judea. It was there that the chief priests, scribes, Pharisees, Sadducees, and those loyal to them remained for the Roman army to attack and decimate in AD 70.

Prior to this Roman invasion, real Jews in Judea, seeing *Jerusalem compassed with armies* (Luke 21:20), recognized that *the abomination of desolation spoken of by Daniel the prophet* (Matt. 24:15) was near. Aware of this and Christ's warnings to *flee Judea,* these Christian Israelites did just that. For this reason, that of the thousands which died in the siege of Jerusalem, there were few if any Christian Israelites among them. This is described by first-century historians such as Flavious Josephus and in older commentaries (Adam Clark's, Matthew Henry's, etc.). Later reference works, those influenced by C. I. Scofield's interpretational notes,[3] have attempted to rewrite history by futurizing these events.

The Kingdom of God Taken from Them

That Yahweh God would dethrone and slay Israel's old covenant religious leaders was also prophesied by Jesus in his parable of the wicked husbandmen (Matt. 21:33-46). The *son* in this parable is symbolic of God's Son, and the wicked husbandmen, of those who would kill the Son. When Jesus finished telling this parable, those to whom it was directed *(the chief priests and Pharisees)* incriminated themselves by saying, *He will miserably destroy those wicked men, and will let out his vineyard to other husbandmen, which shall render him the fruits in their seasons* (v. 41). It was then that Jesus declared:

> Therefore, I say unto you, The kingdom of God shall be taken from you, and given to a nation bringing forth the fruits thereof.   Matthew 21:43

It was when Jesus said that the kingdom, that the administration of God, would be taken from these Old Covenant

---

[3] Scofield Reference Bible, 1909 and later editions.

leaders, that *they perceived that he spake of them,* and *sought to lay hands on him,* but dared not because *they feared the multitude* (vv. 45, 46).

The Judean scribes, Pharisees, and other authorities, those who sought to *lay hands* on Jesus, did not do so for fear of *the multitude,* the multitude of Jews. If as is taught by Judeo-Christian teachers Israel rejected Jesus, why then do they not explain who this multitude was? Instead it seems, we are supposed to assume that *the multitude,* that *the common people,* because they were accepting of Jesus, were not Israelites. This is confusion.

What Advantage Hath the Jew?

What advantage then hath the Jew? Or what profit is there of circumcision? Much every way: chiefly, because unto them were committed the oracles of God. For what if *some* did not believe? Shall their unbelief make the faith of God without effect? God forbid.   Romans 3:1-4 (emphasis mine)

This tells us it was the Judah portion of Israel to whom *were committed the oracles of God* and, therefore, whose responsibility it was to be the first among Israelites to accept the gospel. It also tells us that *some,* not all Jews, *did not believe.* This agrees with what we have read so far, that the first Christians were Jews, that

> The first Christians were Jews.

the church at that time was an Israelitish institution. It was those among Jews who *did not believe* who remained in control of Jerusalem, the temple, and *the oracles of God.*

The sum of these and other aspects of Israel's religion was *the kingdom of God,* the administration of which was to be taken from unbelieving Jews, which it was in AD 70. From that point onward it would be those *bringing forth the fruits thereof* (Matthew 21:43) to whom would be *committed the oracles of God* (the Bible), and who will *inherit the kingdom,* the administration of God at the end of the age. As will be explained in chapters which follow there is a reason why, through the centuries, it has been primarily one people among whom the Bible is found and Christianity propagated.

In Matthew chapter 23 is the longest, most scathing denunciation of anyone in Scripture. Jesus, in an entire chapter, condemns the Judean scribes and Pharisees. What follows are excerpts of his closing statement.

> Ye serpents, ye generation of vipers, how can ye escape the damnation of hell? ...I send unto you prophets, and wise men, and scribes: and some of them ye shall kill and crucify; and some of them shall ye scourge in your synagogues, and persecute them from city to city: That upon you may come all the righteous blood shed upon the earth.... Verily I say unto you, All these things shall come upon this generation. O Jerusalem, Jerusalem, thou that killest the prophets, and stonest them which are sent unto thee, how often I would have gathered thy children together, even as a hen gathereth her chickens under her wings, and ye would not! Behold, your house is left unto you desolate. vv. 33-38

It was shortly thereafter that these corrupt religious leaders would crucify Israel's Messiah. Within three years they had killed Stephen also (Acts 7:59), and true to Christ's words were persecuting Messianic Israelites, were persecuting real Jews, from *city to city.* Chief among these persecutors was one Saul of Tarsus who, prior to his conversion, *made havoc of the church, entering into every house, and haling men and women committed them to prison* (Acts 8:3). It was after his conversion that Saul, renamed Paul, no longer had his former Pharisaical synagogue-of-Satan mind-set.

> Then had the churches rest throughout all Judea and Galilee and Samaria, and were edified; and walking

in the fear of the Lord, and in the comfort of the Holy
Ghost, were multiplied.   Acts 9:31

That the churches throughout Palestine were comprised of
Messianic Israelites is consistent with previous references
to the multitudes of common people who were accepting of
Jesus, when the gospel was preached, to the Jew first (Rom.
1:16; 2:9-10). If the gospel had not been spreading among
Jews, Saul would not have been trying to stop it. Remember,
it was because Jesus was popular with the average Jew that
the Judean authorities conspired to kill him. Had Jews not
been accepting of Jesus he would not have been a major
concern to their leaders.

> For he (Apollos) mightily convinced the *Jews,* and
> that publicly, showing by the scriptures that Jesus
> was Christ (Messiah).
> Acts 18:28 (emphasis, parentheses mine)

What About John 1:11?

Despite what you have just read, dispensational teachers
will counter with, *he came unto his own and his own received
him not.* This, of course, implies that their interpretation
of one verse overrules a plethora of other texts, and even
whole chapters which say the opposite. The rest of the story
is in verse 12, *But, as many as received him, to them gave he
power to become the sons of God, even to them which believe
on his name.* Dispensationalists need to be reminded that
Scripture does not contradict Scripture; interpretations only
do that.

Verse 11, consistent with the principle of noncontradiction, is emphasizing Christ's earthly ministry. This lasted
about three-and-one-half years and occurred in Palestine
only where it was *his own* religious leaders, and their loyalists, who *believed him not.* Verse 12 is a summary of the
gospel as preached in those early years, *to the Jew first.*
This begins in Matthew and continues through much of

Acts. During this time thousands of Israelites, being real Jews, *believed on his name*, and in fulfillment of Isaiah's prophecy were becoming known as Christians. It is now two thousand years later and ironic how millions of their descendants, because they are Christian, assume—they are not Israelites.

The prophet Hosea, writing of Israel, stated: *my people are destroyed for lack of knowledge* (Hosea 4:6). Our nation's decline is the direct result of our lack of knowledge and our disobedience to the Law of the Lord. This problem would be greatly reduced if the clergy would stop telling us that we, of historic Christianity, are not the Israelites referred to in this verse—that someone else is—because they say, "Israel rejected Jesus."

What Did Isaiah Say?

> For unto us a child is born, unto us a son is given: and his name shall be called Wonderful, Counselor, The Mighty God, The everlasting Father, The Prince of Peace. Of the increase of his government and peace there shall be no end.   Isaiah 9:6-7

The birth of Jesus and his acceptance by Israelites were clearly foretold by the prophet Isaiah. Chapters 41-66, especially, attest to this. The same, however, describe his rejection by a portion of God's covenant people. These verses, along with John 1:11 and a few others, are used by the dispensational establishment to promote the idea that most Israelites rejected Jesus. Having established this interpretation, these verses are then repeated and emphasized to the exclusion of a majority of texts which say the opposite of their John 1:1 interpretation.

It is unfortunate that most Christians, because they read Scripture loosely, if at all, are often not aware when someone is not telling them the rest of the story. They may become suspicious at times but usually step back into line when their dispensationally trained pastor or Christian talk show host reminds them that *his own received him not.*

The Lord, the Redeemer of Israel

Remember these, O Jacob and Israel; for thou art my servant: I have formed thee; thou art my servant: O Israel, thou shalt not be forgotten of me. I have blotted out, as a thick cloud thy transgressions, and as a cloud, thy sins: return unto me; for I have redeemed thee. Sing, O ye heavens; for the Lord hath done it: shout, ye lower parts of the earth: break forth into singing, ye mountains, O forest, and every tree therein: for the Lord hath redeemed Jacob, and glorified himself in Israel.   Isaiah 44:21-23

Jesus, the Redeemer of Israel

And the Redeemer shall come to Zion, and unto them that turn from transgression in Jacob, saith the Lord. As for me, this is my covenant with them, saith the Lord; My spirit that is upon thee, and my words which I have put in thy mouth, shall not depart out of thy mouth, nor out of the mouth of thy seed, nor out of the mouth of thy seed's seed, saith the Lord, from henceforth and for ever.   Isaiah 59:20-21

Isaiah, speaking of *them which turn from transgression in Jacob,* declared that God's Spirit, that the words which he put into the mouths of these repentant Israelites, would not depart from them or their descendants *forever.* This clearly tells us that the Israelite descendants of those first Christians would continue, in an unbroken line, as the nucleus of the church and the custodians of God's Word.

Judeo-Christian teachers, when pressed, will admit that the first Christians were Israelites. However, in the next breath they will say that Christianity fizzled out among their descendants. When this supposedly happened they do not say, only that it must have happened. This, of course, is pure conjecture, but a position they must hold because of whom they identify as Israel.

Acceptance Foretold by Zechariah and Simeon

In chapters 1 and 2 of Luke is a most beautiful introduction to the birth of John the Baptist and Jesus. Of John Luke wrote: *and many of the children of Israel shall he turn to the Lord their God...to make ready a people prepared for the Lord* (2:16, 17). It was Israelites who, as a result of John the Baptist, would be a people prepared for the coming of Jesus the Messiah. Was John a failure? Were Israelites in Palestine so unprepared for the coming of their Messiah that they rejected Jesus? Of him Luke wrote:

> He shall be great, and shall be called the Son of the Highest: and the Lord God shall give unto him the throne of his father David: And he shall reign over the house of Jacob forever; and of his kingdom there shall be no end. Luke 1:32-33

How can this be true if, as taught by the Judeo-Christian establishment, Israel rejected Jesus, because, apparently, John the Baptist did not sufficiently prepare them for the coming of their Messiah? Who then did Jesus *reign over,* beginning in AD 33 and since? Is it not, according to Mary's prophecy? Luke recorded it as follows:

> He hath holpen (helped) his servant Israel, in remembrance of his mercy; as he spake to our fathers, to Abraham, and to his seed forever. Luke 1:54-55 (parenthesis mine)

Mary, as did Isaiah, declared it was to Israel, to Abraham, and his seed that God's mercy would extend, in an unbroken line, *forever.* Zechariah, the priest and the father of John the Baptist, also prophesied concerning Jesus and Israel:

And his father Zechariah was filled with the Holy
Ghost, and prophesied, saying, Blessed be the Lord
God of Israel; for he hath visited and redeemed *his
people,* and hath raised up a horn of salvation *for us,*
in the house of his servant David; as he spake by the
mouth of his holy prophets, that we should be saved
from our enemies, and from the hand of all that hate
us; to perform the mercy promised *to our fathers,*
and to remember his holy covenant; the oath which
he sware to our father Abraham.

Luke 1:67-73 (emphasis mine)

It should not be overlooked that when the Scriptures
refer to *us* and *his people* that these words, in the context
of Zechariah's and other prophecies, are specific of God's
Israel covenant people, those with whom the Old and New
covenants were made. Politically correct this is not, but it is
what it is.

And behold, there was a man in Jerusalem, whose
name was Simeon; and the same man was just and
devout, waiting for the consolation of Israel: and
the Holy Ghost was upon him. And it was revealed
unto him by the Holy Ghost, that he should not see
death, before he had seen the Lord's Christ. And he
came by the Spirit into the temple: and when the
parents brought in the child Jesus, to do for him
after the custom of the law, Then took he up him
in his arms, and blessed God, and said, Lord, now
lettest thou thy servant depart in peace, according
to thy word: for mine eyes have seen thy salvation,
which thou hast prepared before the face of all
people; a light to lighten the Gentiles and the glory
of thy people Israel.   Luke 2:25-32

So God's Word tells us that Jesus *hath visited and redeemed*
Israel and that Jesus is *the glory of thy people Israel.* But along
comes an interpretation telling us, "because Israel rejected
Jesus," these prophecies failed.

CHAPTER 5

THE CHURCH, ISRAELITISH OR NOT?

I f, as taught by Judeo-Christian teachers, there was a wholesale rejection of Jesus by Israel, one would expect to find the first Christians described as Canaanites, Edomites, and other nearby non-Israelitish people. This is not the case.

As previously demonstrated, much of Acts is a record of Jews, as many as five thousand at one time (4:4) accepting Jesus and the new Christian covenant. Other references to Jews accepting Jesus are, 5:14; 6:7; 9:31; 11:24-26; 13:43; 14:1; 15:5; 17:12; and 18:4, 8. These culminate with, and are corroborated by Acts 18:28 and 21:20 which say:

> For he (Apollos) mightily convinced the Jews, and that publically, showing by the scriptures that Jesus was Christ.

> Thou seest, brother, how many thousands of Jews there are which believe.

A portion of these Israelites would have been Jews in a national (Judeans) and in a religious sense; others in a religious sense only. It must be emphasized that these were real circumcised-in-heart Jews (Rom. 2:29); they were not the non-Messianic, synagogue-of-Satan type *(them which say they are Jews and are not* [Rev. 2:9; 3:9]).

> This transition, from Jew to Christian, was mostly complete by the end of the second century.

Messianic circumcised-in-heart Jews were *called Christians first in Antioch* (Acts 11:26). That God would call his servant people by *a new name; by another name,* was foretold by the prophet Isaiah (62:2; 65:15). This is why the descendants of those *thousands of Jews* were, in a generation or two, no longer called Jews, but Christians. History proves this transition, from Jew to Christian, was mostly complete by the end of the second century.

It was the Pharisees and their loyalists, *those which believed not* (Acts 17:5) who would cling to *Jew,* to Israel's old covenant name. Their descendants, to the extent that they exist today, would be a small minority among the total population of latter-day Israel. They are not, as claimed by dispensationalists, the only remaining descendants of God's Israel covenant people. This is fallacious and serves no purpose other than to rob the rightful heirs of God's promise to Abraham in Genesis 12:3. This includes, obviously, the latter-day Christian descendants of those *thousands* of Messianic Jews long ago.

Most today who say they are Jews, because they are not Christian, do not qualify as heirs, much less as the sole heirs of God's promise in Genesis 12:3. Whether or not they are Israelites is of no consequence. As Paul explained, *if ye be Christ's then are ye Abraham's seed, and heirs according to the promise* (Gal. 3:29). *If,* as used in this verse, means that the promise is conditional; it applies to Israelites who are Christians, to those who are *Christ's.* Then, only, are they counted as Abraham's seed, *and heirs according to the promise.* We conclude then that the book of Acts identifies the early church as an Israelitish institution.

Hebrews, an Epistle to Christian Israelites

Because the address is in the title, it cannot be argued that the epistle to the Hebrews was written other than to Hebrew-Israelites. This epistle, more than others, explains Israel's transition, from the Old to the New Covenant. In it is a verbatim quotation of Jeremiah's prophecy concerning this new covenant.

> Behold the days come, saith the Lord, when I will make a new covenant with the house of Israel and with the house of Judah.
>
> Hebrews 8:8; Jeremiah 31:31

Note with whom the New Covenant would be made, *the house of Israel and with the house of Judah.* Chapter 8, in great detail, explains and emphasizes that it is Jesus the Messiah who is high priest of this new and *better* covenant. Chapter 9, continuing this theme, explains the superiority of *the blood of Christ* over that of bulls and goats. Chapter 10 further explains how Jesus, *after he had offered one sacrifice for sins forever, sat down on the right hand of God.*

Hebrews, written present in tense and to Hebrew-Israelites, thus refutes the following claims made by the Judeo-Christian dispensational establishment:

1. That their opening line, "Because Israel rejected Jesus," identifies the church as a non-Israelitish institution.
2. That, because they say, "Israel rejected Jesus," the Old Covenant was interrupted and put on hold seven years short of completion.
3. That, because they say, "Israel rejected Jesus," God owes a nation of neo-Pharisees a second chance in some future seven-year period, which they say, completes the Old Covenant dispensation.
4. That this seven-year period, this second chance, will begin immediately after *the Lord himself will*

> *descend from heaven with a shout* (1 Thess. 4:16);
> *at his coming* (1 Cor. 15:23).

5. That Christ, upon descending *from heaven; at his coming,* will immediately go back for seven years during which time the Israelis, acting upon this said-to-be second chance, accept Jesus as Messiah—just before he descends from heaven again—a third time!

Incredibly, these claims are included in dispensationalism, a chain of futuristic interpretations that was unknown to the early church fathers and Protestant Reformers.

The Mantra of Dispensationalism

Mantra, according to dictionary definition is, "An expression or idea that is repeated, often without thinking about it, and closely associated with something."

In the introduction to his interpretational Bible, C. I. Scofield, commenting on Jesus and Israel, stated, "His rejection by that people."[4] Scofield's modus operandi for identifying Israel has become a mantra and an opening line for dispensationalist-futurist teachers and preachers. They preface sermons, chapters, and entire books by stating, "Because Israel rejected Jesus." This is often followed by a message in which Christians are warned to bless those who currently reject Jesus lest the curses mentioned in Genesis 12:3[5] befall America.

Despite overwhelming evidence to the contrary, and true to the definition of mantra, this teaching that Israel rejected Jesus two thousand years ago is accepted without question by most evangelicals. They do not, in the Berean spirit, *search the Scriptures* (Acts 17:11) whether it is so. More will

---

[4] Scofield Reference Bible, p. 6, 1917 edition.
[5] "And I will bless them that bless thee, and curse him which curseth thee."

be said regarding the dubious C. I. Scofield in chapters to follow.

James, an Epistle to Christian Israelites

James, another of the general epistles, was written hundreds of years after the deportation of ten-tribed Israel and two-tribed Judah. It is addressed, and begins, as follows:

> James, a servant of God and of the Lord Jesus Christ, to the twelve tribes which are scattered abroad, greeting.   James 1:1

The context of James, like Hebrews, is addressed to Israelites and describes them as a Christian people. This is not argu-able. James was not telling us that the Judean and Galilean Israelites also were *scattered abroad;* only that all twelve tribes were represented among those scattered abroad. Since Israel was prophesied to number *as the sand of the sea* (Hosea 1:10), this would have been in the millions at that time. James knew:

- That the Diaspora, the dispersion of Israel, occurred not when Rome sacked Jerusalem and Judea in AD 70, but in the seventh and sixth centuries BC with the Assyrian and Babylonian invasions and deportations.
- That he and most Palestinian Israelites were descended from the *remnant* of Judahites which returned from Babylon, and that they were not all of Judah, much less all of Israel.
- That the rejection of Jesus by a minority of Israelites did not constitute a wholesale rejection of the Messiah.
- That Jesus was widely received by Israelite laypeople, and who, in fulfillment of Isaiah's prophecy, were becoming known as *Christians.*

This general epistle is proof positive that the New Covenant congregations, i.e., the church, were comprised of those to whom the New Covenant was promised, *the house of Israel and the house of Judah* (Jer. 31:31). James thus refutes the common teaching that "Israel rejected Jesus," the foundation of sand upon which the dispensationalist-futurist interpretation is built.

The First Epistle of Peter

Included with Hebrews and James as one of the general epistles is 1 Peter. It opens as follows:

> Peter, an apostle of Jesus Christ, to the *strangers scattered* throughout Pontus, Galatia, Cappadocia, Asia, and Bithynia. Elect according to the foreknowledge of God the Father, through sanctification of the Spirit, unto obedience and sprinkling of the blood of Jesus Christ: Grace unto you, and peace be multiplied.
>
> 1 Peter 1:1 (emphasis mine)

Do your homework and discover that *strangers scattered* is best understood as Diaspora or, the dispersed of Israel. They were *elect,* a term also indicative of Israelites (*Israel mine elect [Isaiah 45:4]).* That Peter was writing to the descendants of divorced cast-off Israelites in the aforementioned locations is further demonstrated by his reference to Hosea 1:9-10:

> But ye are a chosen generation, a royal priesthood, a holy nation, a peculiar people; that ye should show forth the praises of him who hath called you out of darkness into his marvelous light: Which in time past were not a people, but are now the people of God: which had not obtained mercy, but now have obtained mercy.   1 Peter 2:9-10

Peter was revealing what most evangelicals overlook. He was identifying the Christians to whom he was writing as the Israelites *which had not obtained mercy, but now,* through Israel's Messiah and the New Covenant were obtaining mercy. These were the uncircumcised non-Jew Israelites of the dispersion, those whom Peter and others of the circum-cision (Jews) formerly considered unclean. Nineteen years earlier (AD 41) Peter had been given a vision (Acts 10:9-16) in which common and unclean animals descended from heaven as he heard a voice saying:

> Rise Peter, kill and eat. But Peter said, not so Lord; for I have never eaten anything that is common or unclean. And the voice spake unto him again the second time, what God hath cleansed, that call not thou common. This was done thrice: and the vessel was received up again into heaven.   Acts 10:13-16

Despite the fact that Peter, at this point, *doubted in himself what the vision which he had seen should mean* (v. 17), dispen-sationalists, it seems, have no doubt. Upon reading where it says, *rise Peter, kill and eat,* they look no further and declare what God had cleansed were the animals; that it was now okay to eat swine's flesh and other unclean things. But read on and discover that the unclean animals in Peter's vision *(done thrice)* were symbolic of *three men* (v. 19). What God had cleansed was not the animals, it was *three men,* three uncircumcised non-Jew Israelites. It was now okay for Peter and other Jews to eat and otherwise *keep company* with those of the dispersion. As Peter concluded:

> God hath showed me that I should not call any man common or unclean.   Acts 10:28

Thus was the purpose of Peter's vision, a revelation which resulted in an epistle written nineteen years later, to the scattered lost sheep of the house of Israel.

CHAPTER 6

ROMANS, AN EPISTLE TO NON-JEW ISRAELITES

Romans, unlike Hebrews, James, and others, was not written to the church universal; it was written by the apostle Paul to a specific congregation, that in Rome. This epistle more than others is used by dispensationalists to promote the assumption that those whom Paul was writing were a mixture of non-Israelitish people, that they were of the other *families of the earth* (Amos 3:2).

If, according to that Judeo-Christian opening line ("Because Israel rejected Jesus") Christians called Gentiles in this epistle were Edomites, Canaanites, and other non-Israelitish people, there should be multiple witnesses to this in the text. Thus will we identify those whom Paul was writing, not by supposition, but by contextual evidence.

"Gentiles," as used in Romans is #1484 and #1672 in the Greek dictionary of *Strong's Concordance.* Number 1484 is *Ethnos* and the most broadly defined. Plural only, *Ethnos* is translated as *Gentiles, heathen, nation,* and *people.* Number 1672 in Strong's is *Hellen,* which is translated "Greeks" and means, Greeks or Greek-speaking people. In Romans 2:9, 10, and 3:9 only is *Gentiles* from *Hellen.* In all others it is based upon *Ethnos.* We will identify the ethnicity of the *Ethnos,* the Gentiles in this epistle, by following the rules, by interpreting this word, in context.

In its opening chapter Romans provides many clues regarding the ancestry of those to whom it is written. In verse 6 they are described as *the called of Jesus Christ.* Being the *called* of God/Christ was descriptive of and a promise to Israel, one repeated extensively in chapters 41-66 of Isaiah. The prophets are replete with references describing Israel as the first and primary recipient of grace and salvation through Jesus the Messiah. Chapter 1 tells us these Romans were the descendants of those who:

- Held the truth in unrighteousness (v. 18).
- Were familiar with this truth because, *God hath showed it unto them* (v. 19).
- Once *knew God,* but glorified him not, etc. (v. 21).
- Did not retain God in their knowledge, but became *covenant breakers...who knowing the judgment of God,* were *worthy of death* (vv. 28, 31, 32).

Now, are we to believe that the above is a description of someone outside of God's Israel covenant people, that Paul was describing someone not in possession of God's Word, yet accountable to the same? No! How could they have been *covenant breakers* and have known *the judgments of God* without being the covenant people, without being those to whom the covenants and the judgments of God pertained?

> He showeth his word unto Jacob, his statutes and judgments unto Israel. He hath not dealt so with any nation: and as for his judgments, *they have not known them.* Psalm 147:19-20 (emphasis mine)

This flies directly into the face of seminary and Bible college teachers, those who tell us that Romans was written to a non-Israelitish people, to the other *families of the earth* (Amos 3:2), and that they too know *the judgments of God.* There is every reason to believe that the Roman Christians were descendants of those with whom the Old Covenant was made, i.e., Israelites, *to whom pertaineth...the covenants* (Romans 9:4) those of whom God's Word says:

> You only have I known of all the families of the earth: therefore I will punish you for your iniquities.
>
> Amos 3:2

To obey the Law of the Lord *(for sin is the transgression of the law* [1 John 3:4]) was the responsibility of Israel alone. There is no basis in Scripture for the idea that billions of Asian, African, and other non-Israelite *families of the earth* shared equally in this responsibility. Israel's God is not going to punish non-Israelites for breaking a law covenant they were unaware of and were not a signatory to *(sin is not imputed when there is no law* [Rom. 5:13]).

Other clues as to the ancestry of these Christians are found as:

- Abraham our father (4:1).
- Our father Abraham (4:12).
- Abraham, who is the father of us all (4:16).
- By our father Isaac (9:10).

It is standard procedure for dispensational teachers to ignore the above four references. When this fails they will attempt to explain away *our father* by stating this was not in a genetic, but in a spiritual sense only. Dispensationalists will resort to this Replacement Theology[6]-type argument when a literal interpretation disagrees with their agenda.

To Whom Pertaineth?

Since Esau also was descended from Abraham it was necessary for Paul to explain that it was Isaac's descendants only who were:

---

[6] Replacement Theology also is based on the teaching that Israel rejected Jesus. Its proponents claim that a non-Israelitish church has replaced genetic Israel in God's plan.

Israelites; to whom pertaineth the adoption, and the glory, and the covenants, and the giving of the law, and the service of God, and the promises: Whose are the fathers, and of whom as concerning the flesh Christ came, who is over all, God blessed for ever. Amen.   Romans 9:4-5

Before commenting on chapter 9 it is necessary to remind that verse 3 in chapter 3 tells us it was—*some* Jews only who *did not believe.* It was they, not all Jews, of whom Paul was speaking when he said, *I have great heaviness and continual sorrow in my heart...for my brethren, my kinsman according to the flesh* (9:2-3).

Among this writer's collection of Bible translations is a copy of the New King James Version by Thomas Nelson, Inc., Nashville, Tennessee. In it the editors, as a heading for chapter 9, use that Judeo-Christian opening line, "Israel's Rejection of Christ." If this is true, who accepted Him? If this is true, why did the writer of Acts refer to, *thousands of Jews there are which believe*? Why do Hebrews, James, and other epistles, written to Hebrew-Israelites, describe them in a Christian, new covenant context? Something is wrong when those who know better find reason to interpret the meaning out of language. Romans 3:4 tells us, *let God be true, but every man a liar.* Whether they know it or not, this is what editors and seminary professors are when they repeat that opening line, the mantra of dispensationalism.

Having stated in verse 4 that it was *Israelites; to whom pertaineth,* Paul then explained that, *Neither because they are the seed of Abraham are they all children but, in Isaac shall thy seed be called* (9:7). If, who he was writing, included the descendants of Esau (Edomites), Paul would have described them also as *children* and *called.* He did not. Instead, and contrary to everything you were told in Sunday school, Paul stated—*these are not the children of God* (9:8).

That it was the descendants of Abraham through Isaac only to whom Paul was writing is also revealed in verse 10 where he refers to, *our father Isaac.* The Bible does not contradict itself. If Paul was not writing to Israelites, he would not have referred to Isaac as *our father.* While there is application for this reference in a spiritual sense also, it is not true that the spiritual voids that which is literal. Because the context proves Paul was writing to Messianic, to Christian Israelites, Isaac was their *father,* in an ancestral, and in a spiritual sense.

> For the children (Esau and Jacob) being not yet born, neither having done any good or evil, that the purpose of God according to *election* might stand, not of works, but of him that calleth; It was said unto her, The elder shall serve the younger. As it is written, Jacob have I loved, but Esau have I hated (loved less). What shall we say then? Is there unrighteousness with God? God forbid. For he saith to Moses, I will have mercy on whom I will have mercy.
>
> Romans 9:11-15 (emphasis, parentheses mine)

Election, in Christian theology, is a term describing the process wherein God calls, or chooses, certain people over others, hence the term, "chosen people."

Most of us are, or should be, familiar with the call of Abraham, a theme which begins in the twelfth chapter of Genesis and continues through Revelation. Abraham was *called* by God for a special purpose. Most of the Bible is about this man and the elect among his descendants. Other *families of the earth* (Amos 3:2) are mentioned, but briefly, and only as they interact with Israel.

God's chosen people were not *chosen,* as some believe, for privilege only. They were chosen, primarily, for a responsibility. This responsibility was to administer a theocracy (*the kingdom of God,* among themselves first; then, with Jesus as their king, to the other *families of the earth.* For this reason, for this responsibility, was the calling and election of Israel.

Because the other *families of the earth* were not *called,* i.e., were not assigned this responsibility, there is no reason to believe that God will punish them equally for not keeping it. More will be said about this later. There are those, nevertheless, who object to God's calling of a chosen people on the grounds that this is racially discriminatory, that it is not, apparently, politically correct. Of these Paul asked the following:

> Nay but, O man, who art thou that repliest against God? Shall the thing formed say to him that formed it, why hast thou made me thus? Hath not the potter power over the clay, of the same lump to make one vessel to honor, and another to dishonor?
>
> Romans 9:20-21

Despite this declaration of the sovereignty of God, dispensationalists will (knowingly or otherwise) attempt to make the calling and election of Israel of none effect by quoting verse 24 which says, *he hath called, not the Jews only, but also of the Gentiles.* True, but this does not tell us that these *Gentiles* were non-Israelites. This is supposed only and is predicated on the idea that all Israelites were of Judah and/or were somehow Jews. There is absolutely nothing in the context of Romans 9 or elsewhere in this epistle which identifies these *Gentiles,* these Christians, as Edomites, Canaanites, or other non-Israelitish people. The opposite is true. Paul, in the next five verses, reveals their ancestry by quoting from Hosea 2:23; 1:10 and Isaiah 10:22; 11:15; 28:22; 1:9; and 13:19.

> I will call them my people, which were not my people; and her beloved, which was not beloved. And it shall come to pass, that in the place where it was said unto them, Ye are not my people; there shall they be called the children of the living God. Isaiah also crieth concerning Israel, Though the number of the children of Israel be as the sand of the sea, a remnant shall be saved; for he will finish the work, and cut it short in righteousness: because a short work will the

Lord make upon the earth. And as Isaiah said before, Except the Lord of Sab'-a-oth had left us a seed, we had been as Sodom, and been made like unto Gomor'-rah.   Romans 9:25-29

These verses, from Hosea and Isaiah, contain historical facts and prophetic statements which concern the non-Jew, ten-tribed house of Israel only. They do not apply to any non-Israelite people.

No Respecter of Persons

The Judeo-Christian establishment has no problem with God's calling of an *elect, chosen people,* until that is, Israel is identified correctly. When demonstrated that the first-century church was an Israelitish institution, and that latter-day Israel is, likewise, found within the church, they will invoke their interpretation of Romans 2:10-11. God becomes, suddenly, no respecter of persons. God was, apparently, but ceases to be, when Israel is correctly identified, when that Judeo-Christian opening line is debunked. Following is the pertinent verse:

But glory, honor, and peace, to every man that worketh good, to the Jew first, and also to the Gentile; For there is no respect of persons with God.
                                   Romans 2:10-11

Gentile, as above is translated from Strong's #1672, or *Hellen,* which means Greeks or Greek-speaking people. These verses are comparing Jews to non-Jew Greek-speaking Israelites of the dispersion. They are not telling us there is no longer a distinction between Israel and the other *families of the earth* (Amos 3:2). If this were true, why would Paul use most of chapter 9 to tell us that it is *Israelites; to whom pertaineth* (9:4)? Why did Paul remind those who *repliest against God* that he is sovereign, that he has *power over the clay, of the same lump to make one vessel unto honor, and another unto dishonor* (9:20-21)? Paul, in chapter 9, had the opportunity to tell us that *to whom pertaineth* included the other *families of the earth.* He did not.

Another verse used by dispensationalists in their attempt to make *of none effect* a majority of others is Romans 10-12:

> For there is no difference between the Jew and the Greek: for the same Lord over all is rich unto all that call on him.

Greek, in this verse is from Strong's #1672, or *Hellen,* the same word translated *Gentiles.* Again Paul was comparing Jews to non-Jew Greek-speaking Israelites of the dispersion. These verses are not a comparison of God's Israel covenant people to non-Israelite, other *families of the earth.* Paul was telling Israel that God, as concerning Jews and non-Jew Diaspora Israelites, was no respecter of persons. This, being consistent with the principle of noncontradiction, is the correct interpretation.

Corroborating Evidence

Other verses used by dispensationalists to glorify a certain non-Christian element but ignored when their opening line is debunked are as follows:

> I am the Lord (Yahweh) your God, which have separated you from other people. ...severed you from other people, that ye should be mine.
> Leviticus 20:24, 26 (parenthesis mine)

> For thou art a holy people unto the Lord thy God: the Lord thy God hath chosen thee to be a special people unto himself, above all people that are upon the face of the earth.   Deuteronomy 7:6

> For thou art a holy people unto the Lord thy God, and the Lord hath chosen thee to be a peculiar people unto himself, above all the nations that are upon the earth.   Deuteronomy 14:2

Thou didst separate them from among all the people of the earth, to be thine inheritance.   1 Kings 8:53

Blessed is the nation whose God is the Lord (Yahweh); and the people he hath chosen for his own inheritance.   Psalm 33:12 (parenthesis mine)

For the Lord (Yahweh) hath chosen Jacob unto himself, and Israel for a peculiar treasure.
                  Psalm 135:4 (parenthesis mine)

For the promise that he should be heir of the world, was not to Abraham, or to his seed, through the law, but through the righteousness of faith.
                  Romans 4:13

Judeo-Christian teachers prefer to ignore and/or attempt to make *of none effect* these texts when latter-day Israel is correctly identified, when it is proved that Israelites, Jew and non-Jew, were the nucleus of the church.

Romans 9:4-5 Declares a Church within Israel

Paul lamented the fact that so many of his fellow Pharisees and their loyalists were not among the *thousands of Jews* which believed the gospel. They were his *kinsmen, according to the flesh* and were therefore *Israelites; to whom pertaineth:*

1. *The adoption,* in other words, *the adoption of sons* as explained in Galatians 4:4-7 and others.
2. *The glory,* that which appeared on Mount Sinai and later filled the tabernacle.
3. *The covenants.* These included the Old and the New covenants, those promised to, and made with, the house of Israel and the house of Judah.
4. *The giving of the law.* This was and is the Law of the Lord, Yahweh's perfect law and Israel's divine constitution.

5. *The service of God.* This was the ordinance of worship and sacrifice, in the Old Covenant, and now, as in the New.
6. *The promises.* These included the forgiveness of sin *(sin is the transgression of the law* [1 John 3:4]) and the coming of Jesus the Messiah.

It was *to whom pertaineth* these things whose were the fathers, and of whom as concerning the flesh Christ came. The reason why Paul lamented the unbelief of certain Jews among Israelites was the fact that the *adoption* and the continuation of *the service of God* were conditional. They were conditional upon an Israelite's acceptance of Jesus as the Christ as the prophesied Messiah. Those among Israelites who denied that Jesus was the Christ (that Messiah came *in the flesh* [2 John v. 7]) were cut off from *the promises* and would die in their sins.

As Paul clearly stated, it was Israelites *of whom as concerning the flesh Christ came,* and *to whom pertaineth* these six things. These also contain that which is essential to the New Covenant, to the Christian religion. Since that which *pertaineth* to *Israelites* is also essential to Christianity, it is logical to assume that Romans 9:4-5 points to latter-day Israel as one and the same with Christendom.[7] Who, then, is Christendom if not the Anglo-Saxon, Celtic, Germanic, Scandinavian, and related European people?

One cannot ignore the significance of these people, the world's only ethnic group which, historically, is primarily Christian. Neither, in identifying the covenant people can one reconcile the mantra of dispensationalism with the Christian Israel so clearly described by the writers of Hebrews, James, and others. It cannot be emphasized too strongly that Israel was not a people who denied that Jesus was the Christ *(anti-Christs* [1 John 2:18, 22]). They were not a people who denied that Messiah *is come in the flesh* (1

---

[7] "Christendom," the part of the world where Christianity prevails.

John 4:3; 2 John v. 7). The Judean Pharisees and their loyalists were, but most Israelites were not.

In chapter 10, Paul quotes Joel 2:32:

> For whosoever shall call upon the name of the Lord
> shall be saved.   Romans 10:13

It is unfortunate that most Christians do not go back to the prophets when Paul and others quote them. Joel, in 2:28-32, says this in a prophecy concerning Israel and the remnant among them who would be saved *(the remnant whom the Lord shall call* [v. 32]). Also significant, and which dispensationalists like to ignore, is the fact that Peter, in his address on Pentecost, tells us Joel's prophecy was fulfilled in AD 33. Acts 2:16-21 is clearly saying that Joel's prophecy was fulfilled two thousand years ago. It is not, as futurists teach, yet to be fulfilled in someone today. This teaching is patently false and serves only as a crutch for the idea that Israel rejected Jesus but will accept him some day.

A major stumbling block for most Christians, and why, in their minds, *the other families of the earth* need to *call upon the name of the Lord,* is that if they don't, God is going to sentence them with some horrible punishment, with something worse than death. This is not true, but if it where, would mean that most of the world's deceased are now suffering this fate. We need to remember that it was Israel only of whom God said, *I will punish you for your iniquities* (Amos 3:2). It was they *to whom pertaineth...the law,* who needed therefore to *be saved* from transgressions thereof. More will be said about this later.

The remainder of Romans, interpreted in context, reveals the same. This includes Paul's comparison of the two types of olive trees (11:13-24). Verse 17 says *some,* not all, branches were broken off the good olive tree. These branches were of Judah (Jews). In other words, *some,* not all Jews, because they rejected the gospel, were broken off. Grafted in where *some* of these natural branches were broken off were the saved among non-Jew Israelites. These, as revealed in chapter 1, were the descendants of those who, hundreds of years earlier, had been divorced by God and *scattered abroad among the nations.* It was they whom the context of Romans identifies as wild branches, as grafted in and reconciled back to God, through Jesus and the New Covenant. They were *the lost sheep of the house of Israel.*

CHAPTER 7

CORINTHIANS, GALATIANS, AND EPHESIANS

First Corinthians, an Epistle to Non-Jew Israelites

That these Christians shared Paul's Israelitish ancestry is undeniable:

> Moreover brethren, I would not that ye should be ignorant, how that all *our fathers* were under the cloud, and all passed through the sea; and all were baptized unto Moses in the cloud and in the sea.
>
> 1 Corinthians 10:1-2 (emphasis mine)

Paul identifies Moses and the twelve tribes, those who passed through the Red Sea, as *our fathers*. That there were large numbers of non-Jew Diaspora Israelites in Greece was understood, and was revealed by the Pharisees in a response to Jesus:

> Ye shall seek me and shall not find me: and where I am, thither ye cannot come. Then said the Jews (Judeans) among themselves, Whither will he go, that we shall not find him? will he go unto *the dispersed*

among the Gentiles (Greeks) and teach the Gentiles (Greeks)?

> John 7:34-35 (emphasis, parentheses mine)

The Pharisees knew that most first-century Israelites *(the dispersed)* were outside of Palestine and were not known as Jews. Yes, *the dispersed,* in this context, are also called Gentiles. But, and again, when used in contradistinction to the word *Jew* it does mean non-Jew, but not, necessarily non-Israelite. Also indicating Israelitish ancestry is Paul's instructions to them concerning the Lord's Supper *(the new testament in my blood* [1 Cor. 11:25]). The word *testament* is one and the same and totally synonymous with *covenant*— the New Covenant—that which pertained to, and was made with the house of Israel and the house of Judah. This and other evidence identifies the Corinthian church as Israelitish.

Galatians, an Epistle to Non-Jew Israelites

Paul was writing to the Christian Israelites, earlier described by Peter, as in *Galatia.* It was because they were descended from the divorced cast-off portion of Israel that they were not *of the circumcision.* They had been cut off from the Old Covenant rituals, but were being recovenanted to God through Jesus, high priest and mediator of the prophesied new and better covenant. That these Christians, as was Paul, were descended from Isaac is demonstrated by the following:

> Now we, brethren, as Isaac was are children of the promise.... We are not children of the bondwoman (Hagar), but of the free (Sarah).
>
> Galatians 4:28, 31 (parentheses mine)

The above tells us that the Galatian Christians, being descended from Sarah, were Israelites. As Paul explained in Romans it was to Abraham and his seed, through Isaac only, that the promise was made. For this reason words found in Galatians such as *promises* (3:16), *law* (4:5), *adoption* (4:5), and others should not be interpreted apart from applications of the same in Romans 9:4. This is especially true as concerning *the adoption*:

> When the fullness of time was come, God sent forth his Son, made of a woman, made under the law, To redeem them that were under the *law,* that we might receive *the adoption* of sons. And because ye are sons, God hath sent forth the Spirit of his Son into your hearts, crying Abba, Father. Wherefore thou art no more a servant but a son; and if a son, then an heir of God through Christ.
>
> Galatians 4:4-7 (emphasis mine)

These verses clearly tell us that Jesus was sent *to redeem them that were under the law* (Israelites) *that we* (Israelites) *might receive the adoption of sons.* It was the Galatian Christians also, who were Israelites, and as Paul stated in Romans 9:4, *to whom pertaineth the adoption.* This corroborates with other evidence revealing Galatians as an epistle to the redeemed *lost sheep of the house of Israel.*

Ephesians, an Epistle to Non-Jew Israelites

Ephesus was in Greece where, as the Judean Pharisees stated, many of *the dispersed* (John 7:35) were located. Numerous references in this epistle contain key words and phrases (Example: 2:11-19) which identify these new covenant believers as descendants of the divorced cast-off portion of Israel. Thanks to Jesus and the New Covenant, the middle wall of partition was broken down between the circumcision (Jews) and uncircumcised non-Jew Israelites. The house of Israel and the house of Judah were being made *both one.*

The Ephesian Christians are identified as *you Gentiles* (3:1), but in the Greek it is *Ethnos.* Also translated as heathen, nation, and people, *Ethnos*/Gentiles is so broadly defined that in the following it includes even—Jews:

He loveth our nation *(Ethnos)* and hath built us a synagogue.   Luke 7:5

The Romans will come and take our place and nation *(Ethnos)*.   John 11:48

We conclude, then, that applications of *Gentiles,* to believers at Ephesus, do not identify these Christians as Edomites, Canaanites, or other non-Israelite people. They were the non-Jew *lost sheep of the house of Israel* (Matt. 10:6), the *other sheep I have which are not of this fold* (John 10:16).

CHAPTER 8

THE OTHER FAMILIES
OF THE EARTH

Search the remaining epistles and you will not find conclusive evidence for a first-century church that was other than Israelitish. The disciples took the gospel, the New Covenant message, as instructed, *to the Jew first,* then *to the Greek,* the Greek-speaking, and other non-Jew Israelites of the Diaspora.

Because there is little said about them in Scripture it is hard to speculate regarding roles, reward, or punishment that God might have for noncovenant people, for the other *families of the earth.* We do know, however, what Jesus told the Canaanite woman:

> Then Jesus went thence, and departed into the coasts
> of Tyre and Sidon. And, behold, a woman of Canaan
> came out of the same coasts, and cried unto him,
> saying, Have mercy on me, O Lord, thou son of David;
> my daughter is grievously vexed with a devil. But he
> answered her not a word. And his disciples came and
> besought him, saying, Send her away; for she crieth
> after us. But he answered and said, *I am not sent but*

unto the lost sheep of the house of Israel. Then came she and worshiped him, saying, Lord help me. But he answered and said, It is not meet (fit) to take the children's bread and to cast it to dogs. And she said, truth Lord: yet the dogs eat of the crumbs which fall from their masters' table. Then Jesus answered and said unto her, O woman, great is thy faith: be it unto thee even as thou wilt. And her daughter was made whole from that very hour.
Matthew 15:21-28 (emphasis, parentheses mine)

Because Jesus healed this woman's daughter did not mean that what Paul described in Romans 9:4-5 also pertained to Canaanites. The gospel, when this healing occurred, was being preached to *the Jew first.* Peter's vision was about ten years away, and others at this time, even non-Jew Israelites, were considered unclean by the Judah remnant in Palestine. This was why the disciples, recognizing her as a Canaanite, said *send her away.* Had she been a Jew it is doubtful they would have done this.

This was the real Jesus—not the Messiah of political correctness.

As Paul explained in the ninth chapter of Romans, it was not Canaanites, etc., but *Israelites; to whom pertaineth...and of whom as concerning the flesh Christ came.* Yes, Jesus did heal the Canaanite woman's daughter, but as an act of mercy, and after she sought Him. That he would refer to this woman and her kind as *dogs* is shocking to those not familiar with this and other texts, but it is what it is. This was the real Jesus—not the Messiah of political correctness.

If some who read this are, as the Canaanite woman, not Israelites, do not worry regarding God's plan for your ancestors or you. He will not judge anyone unfairly. He, however, is probably going to judge you based upon your knowledge of His moral standard. If you are reading this book it is probably because your faith in Jesus is greater than many

Israelites. Continue, therefore, after Him in the faith of that Canaanite woman. Follow God's plan to the best of your ability and He will not disappoint you.

Burn-in-Hell Teaching a Stumbling Block

God's calling of Jacob-Israel as opposed to other *families of the earth* would, for most Christians, be easier to accept were it not for a major stumbling block. This impediment is the idea that non-Israelites also need inclusion in the New Covenant, lest they die in their sins and live forever in a burning hell.

That the soul of man is immortal, that people somehow live on after death as a conscious thinking entity is not scriptural, but a pagan concept. Virtually all non-Christian religions use this idea as a basis for much of their teaching. Among certain American Indians it was known as "going to the happy hunting grounds." In Islam it is known as entering paradise, or "heaven." Among the Hindus of India it is taught as reincarnation. It was promoted by the ancient Greek philosophers, and because it appealed to them, was adopted and retained by certain Diaspora Israelites. It is best described as in the familiar phrase, "go to heaven," and variations thereof. Except for those who believe in a teaching called "purgatory," evangelicals and most Christians accept the idea that anyone who does not "go to heaven" will also continue in a conscious state, but—in hell.

The immortal soul and burning hell doctrine increased during the first centuries of Christianity, and by medieval times, was used by Roman Catholicism to facilitate the selling of indulgences. But Europe was freed from this bondage when the printing press and the distribution of Bibles revealed that *the soul that sinneth, it shall die* (Ezekiel 18:4; 20); that *the wages of sin is death* (Rom. 6:23), not eternal life in some burning hell. As God told Adam and Eve, *in the day that thou eatest thereof thou shalt surely die* (Gen. 2:17). They did. They partook of that which was forbidden and were sentenced with death for the first sin. What happened at their death is described as follows:

> His breath goeth forth, he returneth to his earth: in that very day his thoughts perish.   Psalm 146:4

> For the living know that they shall die: but the dead know not anything.   Ecclesiastes 9:5

> For in death there is no remembrance of thee; in the grave who shall give thee thanks?   Psalm 6:5

> If I wait, the grave *(sheol)* is mine house: I have made my bed in the darkness.
> Job 17:13 (parenthesis mine)

> For there is no work, nor device, nor knowledge, nor wisdom, in the grave *(sheol)* wither thou goest.
> Ecclesiastes 9:10 (parenthesis mine)

> David...fell on sleep (died), and was laid unto his fathers, and saw corruption.
> Acts 13:36 (parenthesis mine)

These tell us that the dead, among all people, whether they were good, bad, Israelite, or Canaanite, etc.—are dead. They are not in some conscious, thinking state. Their bodies, in time, return to the dust (the elements) from which they were created.

It is perhaps, for politically correct reasons, that most evangelicals insist that the Gentile Christians in Romans and other epistles were not Israelites; that God was no longer discriminating as He did with the call of Abraham. To exclude, they say, the other *families of the earth* as His *elect* would be contrary to a loving, merciful God. Then, and ironically, they will imply, with their immortal soul teaching, that this same loving, merciful God condemns billions of unsaved, non-Christian people to a punishment worse than death.

Think for a moment. The first Christian missionaries did not reach most of Asia, Africa, and other historically non-Christian lands until fairly recently in church history. Prior to Europeans and their missionaries, billions of these, historically, non-Christian people were born, lived, and died. They did so without Bibles, and outside of God's

> Are all these people, for hundreds and thousands of years now, screaming and writing in pain?

Old and New covenants. It was not possible for them to know, much less comply with scriptural requirements for salvation. Are they, as consistent with immortal soul teaching, really not dead? If not, and because they were outside of God's covenants and plan for salvation, are they in some burning hell? Are all these people, for hundreds and thousands of years now, screaming and writhing in pain? The answer, thank God, is no. They are not being tortured and burned alive because:

- The dead know not anything (Eccl. 9:5).
- Their thoughts perish (Psalm 146:4).
- They, *go down into silence* (Psalm 115:17).

Sheol (Hebrew), translated, *hell, grave,* and *pit* in the King James Version, is descriptive of the nonconscious, oblivious condition in death. Hades, the Greek equivalent in the New Testament, describes the same. The Bible does not contradict itself. All people, good, bad, Israelite, and others are in the above-described condition within minutes of taking their last breath. Jesus also, when he *gave up the ghost,* was in this condition, but for three days only.

What about the Rich Man and Lazarus?

Most Christians like to think they were born with immortality, that all humans, somehow, continue after death as a conscious thinking entity. They prefer to believe that people do not really die, that the soul and/or the body merely, as some say, "change locations." Those who promote this teaching will often cite as "proof" a parable, that of the rich man and Lazarus.

That this is a parable is evidenced by the fact that it occurs in a sequence of parables. To say otherwise, and that the dead are not really dead, is not in harmony with other Scripture texts on this subject. God is not the author of confusion. Scripture does not tell us, *the dead know not anything,* to then contradict this with a literal account of two people who continue after death as thinking, feeling entities. Jesus, in telling this parable, did not contradict a preponderance of Scripture texts which speak clearly on the state of the dead.

To correctly interpret the rich man and Lazarus, one must begin with Luke 16:14-18, a prelude to this story. In verse 17, Jesus, as he did in the Sermon on the Mount (Matt. 5:17-20), began this parable by declaring the perpetuity of the Law of the Lord. He said: *it is easier for heaven and earth to pass, than for one tittle of the law to fail.* Then, to illustrate this point, he tells a story, the moral of which is at the end and therefore related to the prelude:

> Abraham saith unto him, They have Moses (the law) and the prophets; let them hear them. And he (the rich man) said, Nay, father Abraham: but if one went unto them from the dead, they will repent. And he said unto him, If they hear not Moses (the law) and the prophets, neither will they be persuaded (to repent), though one rose from the dead.
>
> Luke 16:29-31 (parentheses mine)

The moral of this story centers, not on the state of the dead, or what punishment is, but on repentance. And repentance, according to our Lord himself, includes hearing *Moses and the prophets.* Moses, in this context, is synonymous with *law,* with the Law of the Lord (Psalm 1, 119, etc.). Not to be confused with the Old Covenant sacrificial and ceremonial law, the Law of the Lord is that which describes the will of God. These are the statutes and judgments. Codified by Moses and explained in the prophets, we are commanded throughout Scripture (Deut. 6:5-9, etc.) to obey these laws *(for sin is the transgression of the law* [1 John 3:4]). Because they are also called commandments we refer to a summary of these laws as The Ten Commandments.

In light of the fact that most immortal soul teachers are also antinomian (antilaw), it is quite likely they are using the idea of literal torture in the rich man and Lazarus as an excuse to divert attention from Christ's warning regarding lawlessness—the real moral in this story.

Lawlessness is also addressed in the Sermon on the Mount, where it is described as a wide gate and a broad way, one which leads those who practice it, to destruction. Lawlessness (*anomia,* i.e., *iniquity*) is the reason why Jesus,

> *Lawlessness...is the reason why Jesus... will say..., I never knew you: depart from me, ye that work iniquity.*

in that day will say to disobedient Christians, *I never knew you: depart from me, ye that work iniquity* (Matt. 7:21). "Iniquity," #458 in the Greek dictionary of *Strong's Concordance* is *anomia.* It is defined as, "illegality, i.e., violation of law, wickedness, iniquity, transgression of the law, unrighteousness."

Most evangelical leaders do not know nor want to acknowledge this. They would have us believe that a pocket New Testament is sufficient; that it contains all a Christian needs to know. This is not true. It disagrees with why we are told *all scripture is...profitable* (2 Tim. 3:16), and with why we are to live by *every word that proceedeth out of the mouth of God* (Matt. 4:4). *All scripture* and *every word* are inclusive of Moses and the prophets; they do not allow for a pocket New Testament only.

VCY America is a Milwaukee, Wisconsin, based Christian radio broadcaster. Heard on the Web and nationwide on over ninety-five stations, it appeals to evangelicals who do not agree with contemporary Christian music and "Christian" rock. Like most broadcasters, however, its programming reflects the go-to-heaven and burn-in-hell idea of immortal soul teachers.

> They have no problem...with billions of people being tortured and burned alive if it means they "go to heaven."

Having challenged them via e-mail regarding this and other teachings, I received a call late one afternoon. It was the station manager, and among other things, he wanted to know why I was trying to tell them (in his words), "there is no hell." When I tried to explain he was misrepresenting my point that there is a hell, but it is not a place of consciousness and torture, his response was, "What about the rich man and Lazarus?" At this point he informed me that he was an ordained minister and began interrupting as I tried to explain that his interpretation of this story does not agree with a plethora of other texts—those which speak clearly on the state of the dead. The interruptions continued as I tried to quote and explain these verses.

The conversation ended when the ordained minister accused me of teaching "soul sleep" and hung up. This was followed by an e-mail informing me I could no longer reach VCY America, that e-mails from my address to theirs had been blocked.

Immortal soul teachers believe this—not because it agrees with Scripture, but because they want to. They have no problem, it seems, with billions of people being tortured and burned alive if it means they "go to heaven."

This writer once attended a Baptist church function featuring a missionary recently returned from Asia. He described one of his converts, a Chinese man, as asking, "Why did your father not come here and warn my father?" This man was heartbroken. Having been told (and convinced) that he must become a Christian or live forever in a burning hell, he concluded (logically) that his deceased father and his ancestors were suffering this fate.

The Judeo-Christian establishment is in gross theological error by insisting that the New Testament Gentile Christians were not of the Diaspora, i.e., that the New Covenant (Jer. 31:31; Heb. 8:6-13) requires inclusion of non-Israelites lest they—"burn in hell." This is blasphemy. The God of the Bible does not sentence billions of past and present non-Israelites to a punishment worse than death. Yahweh, the covenant God of Jacob-Israel, does not condemn billions of non-covenant people to an eternity of torture in the hell of medieval Catholicism. He did not during the Old Covenant; neither does He in the New. Only Judeo-Christian immortal soul teachers do that.

CHAPTER 9

THE RESURRECTION IDENTIFIES ISRAEL

That Israel cannot be, historically, a non-Christian people (today's Pharisees) is proved by the doctrine of the resurrection:

> For I know that my redeemer liveth, and that he shall stand at the latter day upon the earth: and though after my skin worms destroy this body, yet in my flesh shall I see God.   Job 19:25-26

Job's is one of the earliest references to the resurrection. This Old Testament saint knew that someday he would rise from the dust to live again. Daniel, also knowing this wrote: *many of them which sleep in the dust of the earth shall awake* (12:2). Isaiah (25:8) and Hosea (13:14) foretell of this. Portions of these verses are quoted by the apostle Paul in verses 54-55 in 1 Corinthians 15. This chapter is a repeat of 1 Thessalonians 4:13-18, but in greater detail. The following is Jesus on the resurrection:

- Thou shalt be recompensed at the resurrection of the just (Luke 14:14).

- All that are in the graves shall hear his voice...and shall come forth...unto the resurrection of life (John 5:28-29).
- And this is the father's will which hath sent me, that of all which he hath given me I should lose nothing but, should raise it up again at the last day (John 6:39).
- I will raise him up at the last day (John 6:40).
- I will raise him up at the last day (John 6:44).
- Whoso eateth my flesh and drinketh my blood hath eternal life; and I will raise him up at the last day (John 6:54).
- Martha, when told by Jesus, *Thy brother* (Lazarus) *shall rise again* said *I know that he shall rise again in the resurrection at the last day* (John 11:24 [parenthesis mine]).

The apostle Paul, as recorded in Acts 17, *preached unto them Jesus, and the resurrection* (v. 18).... *and when they heard of the resurrection some mocked* (17:32). Appearing before the chief priests and their council Paul stated, *of the hope and the resurrection of the dead I am called into question* (Acts 23:6).... *For the Sadducees say that there is no resurrection* (v.8). *There shall be a resurrection of the dead, both of the just and the unjust* (Acts 24:15); *Touching the resurrection of the dead I am called into question* (v. 21).

> Why should it be thought a thing incredible with you that, that God should raise the dead?   Acts 26:8

Resurrection, to *Inherit the Kingdom*

That the Old and New Testament saints will rise again in bodily form to eternal life is the reward promised throughout Scripture. Interspersed among the many references to this event are the timing (*the last day*) and the location of those after their resurrection. This location is referred to as, *the kingdom..., Thy kingdom..., my kingdom..., kingdom of heaven..., his kingdom..., kingdom of God...,* and *kingdom.*

That these describe one and the same is demonstrated in the following texts:

> And I say unto you. That many shall come from the east and the west, and shall sit down with Abraham, and Isaac, and Jacob, in *the kingdom of heaven.*
> Matthew 8:11 (emphasis mine)

> Ye shall see Abraham, and Isaac, and Jacob, and all the prophets, in *the kingdom of God*, and you yourselves thrust out. And they shall come from the east, and from the west, and from the north, and from the south, and shall sit down in *the kingdom of God.*
> Luke 13:28-29 (emphasis mine)

Matthew and Luke, describing the same event, use the terms *kingdom of heaven* and *kingdom of God* interchangeably. In Matthew 13:11 Jesus refers to *the mystery of the kingdom of heaven.* Mark, referring to the same, wrote *the mystery of the kingdom of God* (4:11). These and other references demonstrate how this *kingdom* will be the location of those who take part in *the resurrection of the just...at the last day.* A correct understanding of this event and the location of the kingdom is important, because among other things, it proves who the latter-day descendants of ancient Israel are and who they are not. This will be explained later.

CHAPTER 10

WHAT AND WHERE IS THE KINGDOM?

For unto us a child is born, unto us a son is given: and the government shall be upon his shoulder: and his name shall be called Wonderful, Counselor, The mighty God, The everlasting Father, The Prince of Peace. Of the increase of his government and the peace of it shall be no end, upon the throne of David, and upon *his kingdom,* to order it and to establish it with judgment and with justice from henceforth even forever. The zeal of the Lord of hosts will perform this.   Isaiah 9:6-7 (emphasis mine)

The Bible, its own best interpreter, tells us *his kingdom* is a type of government: *his government,* of which there will be *no end.* This was the good news, *the gospel of the kingdom* (Matt. 4:23) as taught by Jesus and the New Testament writers.

Integral with this *gospel of the kingdom* is the gospel of grace and salvation. Those who die without these (in their sins) will not rise, as Jesus said, *unto the resurrection of life...at the last day.* No, this does not mean they will be tortured and burned alive forever in the hell of Catholic and dispensational interpretations. It does mean they will not, as Paul stated, *inherit the kingdom of God* (1 Cor. 6:9; Gal. 5:21).

Paul, in using this phrase, reveals that he was preaching the gospel of the kingdom. If, as dispensationalists say, "because Israel rejected Jesus," Paul was preaching another gospel, and to a non-Israelitish people, where is the evidence? Why, instead of using dispensational terminology ("go to heaven") did Paul say, *inherit the kingdom?* Why, as late as AD 62 was Paul:

> Preaching *the kingdom of God,* and teaching those things which concern the Lord Jesus Christ, with all confidence, no man forbidding him.
>
> Acts 28:31 (emphasis mine)

"Go to Heaven," or *Inherit the Kingdom*?

It should be obvious by now that there are those who, not liking *the gospel of the kingdom,* are teaching another, one with a different location and a different reward. Dispensationalists describe this other gospel by using an expression not in the Bible. Repeated often, and without the user thinking about it, this expression has become another mantra among evangelicals.

> You cannot find the popular phrase, "go to heaven," in the King James Version and other actual translations.

One of the best ways to search Scripture is *Strong's Exhaustive Concordance*, in book form, or on the Internet at *blueletterbible.com.* Using Strong's, search the word *heaven.* Do this in the Berean spirit as you search for the word *heaven* preceded by the words "go to," or "get to." You may or may not be surprised when you cannot find the popular phrase, "go to heaven," in the King

James Version and other actual translations. You cannot find these words in this combination because: neither they nor the idea is in the Bible.

Consider again the phrase used by the apostle Paul who, according to dispensationalists, was not preaching the gospel of the kingdom:

> Know ye not that the unrighteous shall not *inherit the kingdom of God?* Be not deceived: neither fornicators, nor idolaters, nor adulterers, nor effeminate, nor abusers of themselves with mankind, Nor thieves, nor covetous, nor drunkards, nor revilers, nor extortioners, shall *inherit the kingdom of God.*
> 1 Corinthians 6: 9-10 (emphasis mine)

What an opportunity this was for Paul to use the phrase "go to heaven." He did not. Consistent with Corinthians is Paul's warning to the Galatian church regarding these same sins. He wrote: *they which do such things shall not inherit the kingdom of God* (Gal. 5:19-21). The following is a comparison of Scripture to the dispensational go-to-heaven interpretation:

> Know ye not that the unrighteous shall not *inherit the kingdom of God?*
> 1 Corinthians 6:9 (emphasis mine)

> Know ye not that the unrighteous shall not go to heaven?   Dispensational teachers

Ask any dispensational teacher regarding why they substitute "go to heaven" for *inherit the kingdom* and invariably their excuse will be that it is another expression for the same. By this they are implying that Paul also, was locating the kingdom as in heaven.

On more than one occasion this writer has heard Brannon Howse of Worldview Radio quote Jesus as saying, "My kingdom is not on this earth." The pertinent verse is John 18:36 wherein Jesus said, *my kingdom is not of this world.*

Kosmos (Strong's #2889), from which *world* is translated, means order or arrangement. Jesus was telling us that this kingdom and his reign therein were not of that world order, but one to come *(at the resurrection, at the last day).* To imply, as do dispensationalists with their go-to-heaven teaching, that the future reign of King Jesus with his resurrected saints will not be on earth contradicts the following Scriptures:

> For evil doers shall be cut off: but those that wait upon the Lord, they shall inherit *the earth*...; the meek shall inherit *the earth* and shall delight themselves in the abundance of peace...; Blessed are the meek: for they shall inherit *the earth*...; Thy kingdom come thy will be done *in earth* as it is in heaven...; And hast made us unto our God kings and priests: and we shall reign on *the earth.*
>
> Psalm 37:9, 11, etc., Matthew 5:5; 6:10;
Revelation 5:10 (emphasis mine)

> There shall be weeping and gnashing of teeth, when ye shall see Abraham, and Isaac, and Jacob, and all the prophets, *in the kingdom* of God, and you yourselves thrust out. And they shall come from east, and from the west, and from the north, and from the south, and shall sit down *in the kingdom* of God.
>
> Luke 13:28-29 (emphasis mine)

Matthew, referring to the same event (8:11-12), describes the kingdom as, *of heaven.* Dispensationalists, by implying that *of* means "in," thus create the illusion of contradiction. Not liking *the gospel of the kingdom,* and wanting instead to "go to heaven," they are willing to create a contradiction of the Word of God.

When Brannon Howse, the aforementioned talk show host, was e-mailed reminding him he was misquoting Jesus, that John 18:36 does not locate the kingdom as in heaven, his defense was Matthew's *kingdom of heaven. Of,* as in *kingdom of heaven,* means the same as *of* in the kingdom *of* God. The word is used by the Bible writers in a possessive sense. In no way does *of* describe the kingdom *of God...of heaven,* as in heaven. One can only get this idea by reading it into the text (because one wants to believe it).

That Luke and Matthew considered these expressions as totally synonymous is not arguable. The kingdom, *of God..., of heaven,* is one and the same with *my kingdom (I and my Father are one).* This kingdom is that which Jesus said angels would gather out of: *all things which offend and them which do iniquity* (Matt. 13:40-41). It is not, therefore, in heaven.

If, as implied by dispensationalists, this kingdom (the location of our eternal reward) is in heaven, how, as the Scriptures clearly teach, can unsaved people and *things which offend* (unrighteous laws, etc.) be there to be removed at the end of the world (age)? This is confusion.

We are told in Matthew's gospel that Jesus *went about all Galilee, teaching in their synagogues, and preaching the gospel of the kingdom* (4:23). We are also told to *search the scriptures* to *seek first the kingdom of God.* Please do so in a prayerful manner and you will discover that *the gospel of the kingdom,* the message taught by Jesus and the New Testament writers, does not agree with the go-to-heaven gospel of dispensational teachers.

The following comment is that of a well-known eighteenth-century evangelist:

> It is indeed generally supposed that the souls of good men, as soon as dislodged from the body go directly to heaven, but this opinion has not the least foundation in the oracles of God.
> John Wesley (1703-1791), Founder of Methodism

Wesley's pronouncement is difficult to accept if all one has heard (or wants to believe) is a misconception, a kingdom that is not on earth. Jesus, when referring to the reward of the Old Testament and New Testament saints, repeatedly stated, *I will raise him up at the last day.* He could have said "go to heaven when he dies," but did not. Not once did he or the New Testament writers use that phrase, nor did they suggest such a reward.

> For the heavens are the Lord's: but the earth hath he given to the children of men.   Psalm 115:16

Did the Thief on the Cross "Go to Heaven"?

Crucified with Jesus were two criminals, both of whom requested that he save them, but each in a different way. Christ's response to the criminal who acknowledged him as *Lord* is often used to promote the idea that this forgiven criminal, upon dying that day, went to heaven.

> And one of the malefactors (criminals) which were hanged railed on him, saying, If thou be Christ, save thyself and us. But the other answering rebuked him, saying, Dost not thou fear God, seeing thou art in the same condemnation? And we indeed justly; for we receive the due reward of our deeds: but this man hath done nothing amiss. And he said unto Jesus, Lord, remember me when thou comest into thy kingdom. And Jesus said unto him, Verily I say unto thee, Today shalt thou be with me in paradise.
> Luke 23:39-43 (parenthesis mine)

Notice how the malefactor who rebuked the other confessed to being worthy of death. He then acknowledged Jesus as *Lord* before making a request stated: *remember me when thou comest into thy kingdom.* He could have said, "when you die and go to heaven," but he did not. Jesus replied by assuring the thief he would be with Him *in paradise.* The question then is, what did Jesus mean by *paradise?* Was it another word for heaven?

To understand this we must recognize that punctuation was not part of the inspired text. The comma inserted between *thee* and *Today* by the translators, is out of place. It should be, not after thee, but after today. Example: "I say unto thee today, thou shalt be with me in paradise." The *today* in the language of that time was added to emphasize, not when, but the certainty of what would happen. In the vernacular we would say, "I'm telling you now, you will be with me in paradise." Some of us might even remember the expression, "I'm telling you now," as the lyrics and title of a 60s era song by a British musical group called Freddie and the Dreamers.

The following is Christ's reply to the criminal, but as in the Revised Standard Version, and with the comma moved and parenthesis added:

> Truly, I say to you today (now), you will be with me in paradise (the kingdom).
> Luke 23:43 (RSV, comma moved, parenthesis mine)

In Bullinger's *The Companion Bible* (published by Zondervan), Dr. Bullinger's notes on Luke 23:43 explain this punctuation error and resultant misinterpretation. Included in these notes are those referring the reader to Ecclesiastes 2:5 and Revelation 2:7 and 22:1-2 regarding what Jesus meant by *paradise.* As Bullinger explains, it was not applied as another word for heaven; rather, it describes a restored Garden of Eden.

To imply, as do immortal soul teachers, that *paradise* was and is, in heaven, creates multiple contradictions. If for example, the forgiven malefactor was going to be there *today* this would mean that Jesus also, was going to be there *Today.* Consider the following texts and whether, when Jesus died, he went to a paradise in heaven:

> For as Jonah was three days and three nights in the whale's belly; so shall the Son of man be three days and three nights in the heart of the earth.
> Matthew 12:40

> He seeing this before spake of the resurrection of Christ, that his soul was not left in hell, neither his flesh did see corruption.   Acts 2:31

So, when Jesus died on the cross, did he, as dispensationalists imply, "go to heaven"? Or, during those three days and three nights, was he *in the heart of the earth/in hell,* or in other words, in the grave, in the oblivious condition that death is? If, as the Scriptures clearly teach, Jesus was dead and *in hell* (the grave) for three days and three nights, why would the forgiven criminal not be there also? The fact that when Jesus died he was *in hell...in the heart of the earth* for three days and three nights tells us that neither he nor the forgiven criminal were, at the same time, *in paradise.* This means that Jesus and the malefactor were not, as immortal soul teachers say, "in heaven."

This writer was once the recipient of a house call by a local Baptist minister. A seminary graduate, as are most evangelical preachers, this man, upon hearing explained that the forgiven criminal did not go to heaven, reluctantly agreed. He admitted that the malefactor and Jesus were, after death, *in hell,* but as he sheepishly stated, "on the paradise side of hell." Was the preacher taught in seminary that there is a paradise side of hell, a purgatory? Was this idea created as a backup for immortal soul teaching, for when something which people want to believe is debunked? This would be a reasonable conclusion.

If, according to immortal soul teachers, the thief and Jesus did not really die, but merely "changed locations," how did Jesus pay the penalty for sin? *The wages of sin is death* (Rom. 6:23). For Jesus to pay this *death* penalty he had to be dead— as Scripture defines death. This means that He knew *not anything* (Eccl. 9:5); His thoughts *perished* (Psalm 146:4); He went *down into silence* (Psalm 115:17); He was as *them which are asleep* (1 Thess. 4:13, etc.). But, on the third day God His Father raised Him from this condition.

The forgiven criminal was not raised, but remains. He will remain among *them which are asleep* until the day he is resurrected. On this day, when his thoughts and being resume, it will seem as though his death on the cross occurred just moments before. This is

> *Them which are asleep,* because they know *not anything,* will not know if they have been dead one minute or one thousand years.

because, in death there is no concept of time; *them which are asleep,* because they know *not anything,* will not know if they have been dead one minute or one thousand years. There is, for practical purposes, no concept of time between one's last conscious moment and their reawakening on resurrection day. Hallelujah!

Scripture does not contradict Scripture; go-to-heaven interpretations do. If, for example, the apostle Paul thought that the kingdom was in heaven, that the saints were immortal and go there immediately upon death, why did he write the following?

> If after the manner of men I have fought with the beasts at Ephesus, *what advantageth it me, if the dead rise not?* Let us eat and drink; for tomorrow we die.
>
> 1 Corinthians 15:32 (emphasis mine)

Paul, preaching the doctrine of the resurrection, is telling us there is no go-to-heaven-type reward between death and resurrection. He was teaching what is clearly stated in the rest of Scripture, that the dead in Christ are in a state of sleep. In saying, *if the dead rise not...eat and drink; for tomorrow we die,* he was emphasizing the total lack of consciousness or reward between the death of a believer and bodily resurrection *at the last day.* Not until then is death, the last enemy, *destroyed* (1 Cor. 15:26, 54-55). But some will say, "Jesus said our reward is in heaven." True, but he did not say we go there to get it. Revelation 22:12 says He will come to us (*I come quickly; and my reward is with me*).

> For if we believe that Jesus died and rose again, even so them also which sleep in Jesus will God bring with him (raise as Jesus was raised).... For the Lord himself shall descend from heaven with a shout, with the voice of the archangel, and with the trump of God: and the dead in Christ shall rise first.
>
> 1 Thessalonians 4:14, 16 (parenthesis mine)

Why are the saints referred to as, *the dead in Christ* if, according to the go-to-heaven crowd, they are not really dead but alive and in the same place Jesus will descend from? Is this not confusion? And no, *bring with him* is not a reference to their location. It's old English for "raise as him," or, as in the Fenton translation, *restore with him.*

It is ludicrous for the dispensationalist to suggest that *bring with him* locates deceased Christians as in heaven prior to the promised resurrection. In addition to contradicting scores of other Scripture texts, this interpretation ignores verse 17 which says the dead in Christ do not meet him in the air, and are not therefore *ever with him* until he descends from heaven. The go-to-heaven crowd's interpretation of *bring with him* is but another example of how they are willing to create the illusion of Bible contradiction when they need a crutch for wishful thinking.

Also on the resurrection, but with more detail, is chapter 15 of 1 Corinthians:

> Behold, I show you a mystery; we shall not all sleep, but we shall all be changed..., at the last trump...: the dead shall be raised incorruptible, and we shall be changed.... So when this corruptible shall have put on incorruption, and this mortal shall have put on immortality, then shall be brought to pass the saying that is written (Isaiah 25:8); death is swallowed up in victory, O death, where is thy sting? O grave, where is thy victory (Hosea 13:14)?
>
> 1 Corinthians 15:51-52, 54-55 (parentheses mine)

Again, if Paul were a dispensationalist he could have described the dead in Christ as other than dead, as other than in the grave and in a state of sleep. He did not. As Martin Luther asked, "Why is a bodily resurrection necessary to destroy this last enemy if the dead in Christ are not really dead, but alive and in heaven?" What Luther objected to was the false immortal soul teaching, a pagan idea. It is easily recognized in the phrase, "go to heaven," the second mantra of dispensationalism.

It is not necessary to explain other Scripture texts used by go-to-heaven teachers in their attempt to prove this idea. None of these contradict God's Word, on the location of His kingdom, and/or the state of the dead. Interpretations only do that.

CHAPTER 11

"RAPTURE" OR RESURRECTION?

T hat the dead in Christ of all ages would rise from the dust to eternal life in the kingdom of God on earth was written in the prophets, preached by Jesus, and repeated in the New Testament epistles. This future event is made possible by the grace of God through the death, burial, and resurrection of His Son, Jesus the Messiah. Referred to in Revelation 20:5-6 as *the first resurrection,* this event is also described in 1 Thessalonians 4:13-18 and again in 1 Corinthians 15 but in greater detail. The early church fathers, the Protestant Reformers, and virtually all Christians prior to 1900 correctly termed this for what it is, *the resurrection.* It was not until the planting of C. I. Scofield's[8] interpretational notes among evangelicals that certain among them began calling this future event "the rapture."

One of the first training centers to promote pretribulation "rapture" teaching was Moody Bible Institute. Originally allowed as an alternative interpretation only, it is now

---

[8] Read *The Incredible Scofield and His Book* by Joseph M. Canfield, or see Web site, Scofield: The Man Behind the Myth, a review of the same, *http://poweredbychrist.homestead.com/files/cyrus/scofield.htm.*

taught there and elsewhere as fact. Among the earlier and more enthusiastic proponents of this interpretation was the late evangelist Harry Ironsides. In later years, however, he admitted there were problems ("full of holes") with the pretrib timing and seemed to regret an inability to change things in his books. "Rapture" teaching did not become widespread until the name *Israel* was hijacked by a nation of neo-Pharisees in old Palestine. There is a reason why those who support Talmudic Zionism change the theme in 1 Thessalonians 4:13-18 and 1 Corinthians 15 from that of *the resurrection* to their rapture, go-to-heaven interpretation.

Strong's Exhaustive Concordance, which lists each occurrence of every word in the King James Bible, does not list "rapture." *Nave's Topical Bible*, first edition, 1904, does not list it as subject matter. *Halley's Bible Handbook*, as late as the twenty-fourth, 1965 edition, does not use this word in commenting on 1 Thessalonians 4:13-18 and 1 Corinthians 15. In 1974, seventy years after the original, S. Maxwell Coder took the liberty of revising *Nave's Topical Bible*. Surprise, in it, and applied to 1 Thessalonians 4:13-18 and 1 Corinthians 15—is "rapture."

Beginning with *The Late, Great Planet Earth*, the number one nonfiction best seller of the 1970s, prophecy author Hal Lindsey launched the rapture interpretation into recognition with a series of books, each selling in the millions of copies. Since then titles such as the *Left Behind* series, in book and in movie form, have kept evangelicals focused on the idea that 1 Thessalonians 4:13-18 and 1 Corinthians 15 describe "a rapture" of Christians to heaven. It is amazing how a word, so conspicuously absent in the first 1,900 years of church history, was so quickly accepted, and as the dictionary describes mantra, "without thinking about it."

Based upon the idea that Israel rejected Jesus, and another tenet of dispensationalism, is that the gospel of the kingdom (God's theocratic program with Israel) was interrupted and put on hold. In its place, they say, is another, a go-to-heaven-type gospel. Based upon teaching that the Gentile Christians were not Israelites, this other gospel was open, they say, to those who were formerly *without Christ, being aliens from the commonwealth of Israel, and strangers from the covenants of promise, having no hope, and without God in the world* (Ephesians 2:12). That's right, whereas these said to be non-Israelites were formerly excluded from promises to *inherit the kingdom...at the last day,* they are now the recipients of a reward dispensationalists call, "go to heaven/get to heaven." This, they say, is why Christians do not inherit the kingdom with Jesus at the last day, but instead, "go to heaven." As the teaching goes, this occurs immediately upon death, or if the believer is yet alive, when Jesus *descends from heaven* as per 1 Thessalonians 4:13-18 and 1 Corinthians 15 (what dispensationalists now call "the rapture").

As the interpretation goes, immediately following this event, will resume the said to be seven years remaining in the Old Covenant dispensation. During this time, this convenient second chance, a certain non-Christian element is said to get right with God and accept Jesus—just before he descends from heaven again—a third time. This, according to dispensationalists, is when the beneficiaries of their opening line, these historically non-Christian people inherit, with Jesus, the kingdom of God.

"Millennial," Another Mantra

Similar to "rapture" is "millennium." It is perhaps by design that dispensational teachers describe certain events and time periods in Scripture by using words which are not.

As previously demonstrated, when Paul wrote to Israelites of the dispersion, he could have used the dispensational expression, "go to heaven," but did not. Unlike dispensationalists, he did not teach that "real Christians don't really die"; that they merely "change locations." The word *kingdom* and the expression *kingdom of God* are found throughout Paul's epistles.

Also found in these writings, those which dispensationalists say are addressed to non-Israelites, are warnings that certain sinners will not *inherit the kingdom of God.* This is a problem for those who teach that God's program for the church was not to inherit the kingdom of God; that instead, we "go to heaven." Dispensational teachers do not like to be reminded that Paul's use of the phrase, *inherit the kingdom of God,* is but one of many proofs which identify the *Ethnos* and *Hellen,* those to whom he was writing, as Israelites, as non-Jew Israelites.

Jacob, according to Genesis 32:28, was renamed *Israel,* a name which means, "prince with God," or "ruling with God." To rule and reign with God (Jesus) in the kingdom of God was a promise pertaining to Abraham, Isaac, Jacob-Israel, and his descendants. This was the reward Jesus referred to when he said, *ye shall see Abraham, Isaac, and Jacob, and all the prophets in the kingdom of God* (Luke 13:28-29). It was they, and their descendants (through Jacob only), of whom it was promised would *inherit the kingdom of God.* It is they, God's Israel covenant people, who are destined to rule and reign with Jesus, *over the nations* (Revelation 2:26); as *kings and priests...on the earth* (5:10); in, as Paul said, *the kingdom of God.*

This was and is God's promise to Israel, that the righteous among them would rule and reign with Jesus, when *the government shall be upon his shoulder* (Isaiah 9:6), when *the increase of his government and peace there shall be no end* (9:7). Called, *the gospel of the kingdom* (Matthew 4:23, etc.), this was the good news, the message preached by Jesus and the New Testament writers, Paul included.

Dispensationalists, when not preaching their go-to-heaven gospel, will admit there is a time when Jesus will rule on earth. But unlike the apostle Paul they seldom call this the kingdom of God. Their preferred term for this time is "millennium," or "millennial reign of Jesus." This age, according to dispensationalists and their charts, will begin seven years after what they call "the rapture." As the interpretation goes, it is between "the rapture" and "the millennium" that a certain non-Christian people convert en masse to Christianity—just before Jesus descends from heaven again—a convenient third time. It is then, say dispensationalists, that those said to be Israel rule and reign with Jesus— over resurrected saints, in they say, "the millennium," or "the millennial kingdom."

Are you catching on? Someone, by calling it "the millennium," is trying to smokescreen the fact that the beneficiaries of their opening line will not be among *the dead in Christ* and cannot therefore *inherit the kingdom of God.* First, they tell us that Christians (i.e., the church) "go to heaven" because someone else will inherit the kingdom of God. Then, to focus attention away from the fact that Paul's epistles do not teach this they avoid the scriptural term *kingdom of God* and call it "the millennium," or "the millennial reign" and variations thereof.

From there they continue to divert attention away from the kingdom of God by referring to "postmillennial, amillennial, premillennial," and other terms derived from the word millennium. Seminary and Bible college teachers are pressured to do this in an attempt to confuse, to divert attention from the fact that the beneficiaries of their opening line cannot inherit the kingdom and are not therefore Israel. Do not be confused when these teachers substitute "millennium" for *kingdom of God.* We should always raise a red flag when someone is avoiding God's Word in its original context.

Why They Change the Resurrection Theme

There is a reason why dispensationalists have abandoned the classical resurrection theme in the following for a go-to-heaven type interpretation they call "the rapture."

> For the Lord himself shall descend from heaven with
> a shout, with the voice of the archangel, and with the
> trump of God: and the dead in Christ shall rise first:
>
> 1 Thessalonians 4:16

We will expound upon this verse by recognizing the Bible
as its own best interpreter. We will not isolate and interpret this text apart from other texts on the same subject.
Correctly interpreted this verse will be in harmony with
what the prophets and Jesus said regarding the resurrection. In this spirit, that of noncontradiction, consider the
following.

- Three times, one each in the preceding three
  verses, are the dead in Christ referred to as,
  not in heaven, but *asleep...*, *sleep in Jesus...,* and
  asleep.
- This verse, as are those on this subject in
  Isaiah, Daniel, and Hosea, would be prophetic
  of *Israelites; to whom pertaineth* this and other
  promises (Romans 9:4).
- Jesus, (*I am not sent but unto the lost sheep of the
  house of Israel* [Matt. 15:24]) when describing
  the resurrection of the just...at the last day was
  speaking to *Israelites; to whom pertaineth.*
- This event will occur, not as a rapture seven years
  before the last day, but as Jesus stated, *at the last
  day* (John 6:39; 40, 44, 54).
- This resurrection of the just, *at the last day,* is
  what John later referred to as *the first resurrection* (Rev. 20:5-6).
- The saints who rise in this *first resurrection...at
  the last day,* include those *which had not worshiped
  the beast, neither his image, neither had received
  his mark upon their foreheads, or* in *their hands:
  and they lived and reigned with Christ a thousand
  years* (Rev. 20:4).

> Blessed and holy is he that hath part in the first resur-
> rection; on such the second death hath no power, but
> they shall be priests of God and of Christ, and shall
> reign with him a thousand years.   Revelation 20:6

The go-to-heaven idea, that which dispensationalists read into 1 Thessalonians 4:16, is not in harmony with what the prophets and Jesus taught regarding the location (earth) and role (rulers with God) of resurrected saints. This is why dispensational teachers prefer to describe this event by calling it "the rapture." It is done for the same reason they substitute "millennium" for *kingdom of God.* They use these substitutes to confuse, to prevent us from recognizing interpretations (theirs) which are not in harmony with what the prophets and Jesus said regarding the resurrection and the kingdom of God. It is also done out of a need for another error, one designed to cover the first. Having identi-fied Israel falsely, as apart from the church, dispensational-ists are trying to fit the wrong people into God's plan. In so doing they create all manner of confusion and contradiction.

First Thessalonians 4:17 does say that *we which are alive and remain shall be caught up together with them in the clouds, to meet the Lord in the air,* but in this context, what does it mean *to meet?* To understand this we must compare the Greek word *Apantesis* (Strong's #529) from which *meet* is translated and as it is used in other texts. The following shed light on what Paul intended to convey when writing *to meet.*

- Went forth to meet the bridegroom (Matt. 25:1; 6).
- Went forth to meet him (John 12:13).
- They came forth to meet us (Acts 28:15).

To meet, in this sense, means to meet and return with. The residents of a city, when visited by the president of the United States, go forth "to meet" him at the airport. When someone important is coming to your house and you see them approaching, you go forth "to meet" them. This is an act of respect; a method of greeting. It does not mean that those whom we go forth "to meet" turn around and go back where they came from. Neither is there anything in the context of 1 Thessalonians 4:13-18 telling us that Jesus will go back to heaven when the dead in Christ and those alive in the same *are...caught up...to meet the Lord in the air.* These resurrected and translated saints rise up, but no higher than *the clouds.* From there they escort Jesus back to earth to rule and reign with him in the kingdom of God, *And so shall we ever be with the Lord* (v. 17). This, *the kingdom of God,* is what we pray for when saying, *Thy kingdom come. Thy will be done in earth as it is in heaven* (Matt. 6:10).

The Resurrection in 1 Corinthians 15

Chapter 15 of 1 Corinthians is a repeat of 1 Thessalonians 4:13-18, but in greater detail. Paul, having explained the resurrection of Christ, asked, *how say some among you that there is no resurrection of the dead?* (v. 12). Then, using Christ's resurrection as a pattern, he explained God's promise of the same for the dead in Christ *those who are fallen asleep* (v. 6).

> For as in Adam all die, even so in Christ shall all be made alive. But every man in his own order: Christ the first fruits; afterward they that are Christ's *at his coming.* vv. 22-23 (emphasis mine)

> Behold, I show you a mystery; We shall not all *sleep* but we shall all be changed, In a moment, in the twinkling of an eye, at the last trump: for the trumpet shall sound, and the dead shall be raised incorruptible, and we shall be changed.
> vv. 51-52 (emphasis mine)

This, the first resurrection, is what Jesus promised when he said, *I will raise him up at the last day.* Those who take part in this will awake from their long sleep with:

- A spiritual body (v. 44).
- Incorruption (v. 53).
- Immortality (v. 54).

We which are alive and remain unto the coming of the Lord (1 Thessalonians 4:15) will be *changed* (translated) into this same body and being. This is necessary because *flesh and blood cannot inherit the kingdom of God* (1 Cor. 15:50). Note how verse 50 reads, *inherit the kingdom of God.* Paul, in other words, was preaching the gospel of the kingdom. He was not preaching another. You cannot find dispensational terms such as "rapture" and "go to heaven" in these verses. Interpretations only, they are used to confuse us regarding the timing and purpose of the first resurrection. This event will occur:

- *At his coming* (v. 22; 23), not as a rapture seven years before.
- *At the last trump* (v. 52), not as a rapture seven years before.
- *At the last day* (Jesus), not as a rapture seven years before the last day.

Blessed and holy is he that hath part in the first resurrection: on such the second death hath no power, but they shall be priests of God and of Christ, and shall reign with him a thousand years.   Revelation 20:6

Thus is the first resurrection described in 1 Thessalonians 4:13-18, 1 Corinthians 15, and Revelation 20:4-6. When this occurs, the dead in Christ and those alive in the same will be changed, from our natural flesh and blood body, to that which is spiritual, incorruptible, and immortal. Without these characteristics, one would not be fit to inherit the kingdom of God with Jesus *at his coming.*

In My Father's House

The following is another text often used as support for "rapture" and go-to-heaven teaching. To remind the reader of where Jesus will be when he comes *again,* parentheses have been added.

> Let not your heart be troubled: ye believe in God, believe also in me. In my Father's house are many mansions: if it were not so, I would have told you. I go (to heaven) to prepare a place for you. And if I go and prepare a place for you, I will come again (to earth), and receive you unto myself; that where I am (on earth), there (on earth) ye may be also. And wither I go ye know, and the way ye know.
>
> John 14:1-3 (parentheses added)

When Jesus said, *my Father's house,* did he mean heaven? No, this is assumed only. Consider other texts wherein are the words *my Father's house.*

- Make not my Father's house a house of merchandise (John 2:16).
- He entered into the house of God and did eat the showbread (Matthew 12:4).
- Behave thyself in the house of God, which is the church of the living God (1 Timothy 3:15).
- For the time is come that judgment must begin at the house of God (1 Peter 4:17).
- And having a high priest over the house of God (Hebrews 10:21).

Here are five witnesses, all of which tell us *my Father's house* is not in heaven. The first two, because they were applied prior to the New Covenant, identify the temple in Jerusalem. And, notice how the words *my Father's house* and *the house of God* are used interchangeably. The last three, because they were applied after the New Covenant, went into effect apply, not to the old temple, but to the new temple, *the church of the living God. Mansions* in verse 2 is from *mone* (Strong's #3438) the same Greek word translated *abode* in verse 23. The *mansions* then in *my father's house* are the abodes, the abiding places of *the Comforter, which is the Holy Ghost* (v. 26).

Yes, Jesus would *prepare a place* for those to whom these verses speak. This, however, was *the church of the living God,* the *place* where He would be when He came again as *the Comforter...,* as *the Holy Ghost* (v. 26), and which occurred as recorded in the second chapter of Acts on the day of Pentecost in AD 33. That John 14:1-3 is explained in this light in verses 4 through 26 is revealed by Jesus in verse 27. It is here that he closes by repeating his opening line in chapter 14:

> Let not your heart be troubled, neither let it be afraid. Ye have heard how I said unto you, I go away and come again unto you. If ye loved me, ye would rejoice, because I said, I go unto the Father: for my Father is greater than I. And I have told you before it come to pass, that, when it is come to pass, ye might believe.
>
> John 14:27-29

As explained in chapter 10, Jesus did go unto the Father, but not during those three days after dying on the cross. He went to heaven forty days after his resurrection. This and his coming again as *the Comforter...as the Holy Ghost,* are recorded in the first and second chapter of The Acts of the Apostles.

Thus is there nothing in John 14:1-3 about anyone other than Jesus going to heaven.

Who Is Taken, Who Is Left Behind?

Another text used to promote the rapture/go-to-heaven theory is in Matthew, chapter 24:

> But as the days of Noah were, so shall also the coming of the Son of man be. For as in the days that were before the flood they were eating and drinking, marrying and giving in marriage, until the day that

Noah entered into the ark, And knew not until the flood came and *took them all away;* so shall also the coming of the Son of man be. Then shall two be in the field; the one shall be taken, and the other left. Two women shall be grinding at the mill; the one *shall be taken,* and the other left. Watch therefore: for ye know not what hour your Lord doth come.

Matthew 24:37-44 (emphasis mine)

Who was taken away in Noah's flood? Was it not the unrighteous? *So shall also the coming of the Son of man be...one shall be taken, and the other left.* In Luke 17:20-37, a parallel to Matthew 24:29-44, the same is said. There is nothing in these verses about Jesus going back to heaven. Neither, therefore, are Christians *taken;* they are not taken to heaven in this event. Those *taken* are the unrighteous. How and where are answered in verse 37.

And they (the disciples) answered and said unto him, *Where,* Lord? And he (Jesus) said unto them, Wheresoever the body is, thither will the eagles (vultures) be gathered together.

Luke 17:37 (emphasis, parentheses mine)

Matthew's and Luke's accounts clearly teach it is the righteous—that it is Christians—who are left. They are left and will inherit the kingdom of God with He who, at His coming, is here to stay. That those *taken* (out of his kingdom) are the wicked and the unrighteous is also revealed in the parable of the wheat and the tares:

As therefore the tares are gathered and burned in the fire; so shall it be in the end of this world (age). The Son of man shall send forth his angels, and they shall *gather out of his kingdom* all things that offend, and them which do iniquity (lawlessness); And shall cast them into a furnace of fire: there shall be wailing and gnashing of teeth. Then shall the righteous shine

forth as the sun in the kingdom of their Father. Who
hath ears to hear, let him hear.
　　Matthew 13:40-43 (emphasis, parentheses mine)

Again we are told it is the righteous, that it is Christians, who
are left when the unrighteous, when *the tares,* are gathered
out of his kingdom. This is repeated in the parable of the net:

> Again, the kingdom of heaven is like unto a net, that
> was cast into the sea, and gathered of every kind:
> Which, when it was full, they drew to shore, and sat
> down, and gathered the good into vessels, but cast the
> bad away, So shall it be at the end of the world (age):
> the angels shall come forth, *and sever the wicked from
> among the just.* And shall cast them into the furnace
> of fire: there shall be wailing and gnashing of teeth.
> 　　Matthew 13:47-50 (parentheses, emphasis mine)

Where, in these parables, is the idea it is Christians who are
taken, and to heaven? Where is the idea *the coming of the
Son of Man* is momentarily only, that Jesus will immediately
go back to heaven? Where? Are you catching on? The dispensational establishment, having identified Israel falsely and
needing therefore a second chance for today's Pharisees, is
reading a go-back-to-heaven idea into these texts.

Without a Jesus who goes back to heaven, the seminary
professors would have no place for their futurized seventieth week (Daniel 9:27), the said to be seven years of second
chance. This is why they read into Matthew 24:29-44 and
other texts the idea of a Jesus who goes back to heaven.
It's a weak but a necessary link in a chain of interpretations designed to assist a nation of neo-Pharisees in their
masquerade as Israel.

Think for a moment. If, as you read this page, the Lord
himself would descend from heaven as per 1 Thessalonians
4-16 (the second and last time), who would be resurrected—
with a spiritual body, incorruption, and immortality? Who
would be resurrected—with that required to inherit the

kingdom of God? Would it not be *the dead in Christ?* Since it was Israelites to whom pertaineth this kingdom, that which *the dead in Christ* will inherit, does this not mean Israel would have to be, historically, a Christian people?

Think again. How can, historically, a non-Christian people (the dead in Phariseeism), inherit that which pertaineth to Israel (the kingdom of God) when they will not rise on resurrection day; when they will not obtain the necessary *spiritual body, incorruption,* and *immortality?* It is because they recognize this problem that seminary professors, that the teachers of preachers, change the theme in 1 Thessalonians 4:13-18 and 1 Corinthians 15 from that of the resurrection to their rapture/go-to-heaven interpretation. They need a Jesus who goes back to heaven; they need a Jesus who does not gather out of his kingdom today's Pharisees but leaves them behind—with a second chance.

This, as the interpretation goes, will occur as their said-to-be future seventieth week, that which they say will commence at "the rapture" and end when Jesus descends from heaven again—a third time. They say that it is during the second half of this futurized seventieth week, this second chance, that a nation of neo-Pharisees will accept Jesus and inherit the kingdom of God when He descends from heaven again—a third time.

This is what motivates Judeo-Christian teachers to futurize Daniel's seventieth-week prophecy. Having identified Israel falsely they need a second chance for today's Pharisees.

The Seventieth Week, Future or Fulfilled?

The professors at Dallas Theological Seminary and other dispensational training centers would know that classical Protestant interpretation recognizes Daniel's seventieth-week prophecy as fulfilled two thousand years ago. They know that the rules of language do not allow for *he* in this text as a yet-to-be dictator said to be "the Anti-Christ." The portion in question is as follows:

> And he shall confirm the covenant with many for one week: and in the midst of the week he shall cause the sacrifice and the oblation to cease.... Daniel 9:27

Now, where in this verse is the word anti-Christ? Where, is this evil dictator, who futurists say, will make, then break a covenant with the Israelis? Yes, *he* is the subject of the text, but *he* is a pronoun and must modify a noun. The noun *he* modifies is *Messiah* in verses 25-26. Verse 27 then, is telling us that Messiah, by His own sacrifice, caused the Old Covenant *sacrifice and oblation to cease.* Neither, as some say, can *he* refer to the word *prince* in the phrase, *the people of the prince that shall come shall destroy the city and the sanctuary* (v. 26).

Not only would this be grammatically incorrect, but still, it would not make this prophecy unfulfilled. *The people of the prince that shall come* were the Romans. This identifies *the prince* as Titus, the Roman general who destroyed *the city* (old Jerusalem) and *the sanctuary* (temple) in 70 AD. Jesus, forewarning his disciples of this had said, *And when ye shall see Jerusalem compassed with armies, then know that the desolation thereof is nigh* (Luke 21:20).

That Daniel's seventieth-week prophecy was fulfilled in this way is the position taken in older and respected commentaries (Matthew Henry's, Adam Clarke's, Jamieson, Fausett and Brown's, etc.). Also taking this position were post-Reformation notables such as Charles H. Spurgeon (1834-1892) and others well into the 1900s. The dispensational establishment does not like to admit this. They teach respect for the early church fathers, Protestant Reformers, Spurgeon, and others, but they do not like to admit that none of these men taught a futurized seventieth week. They all taught that *he* in verse 27, is *Messiah* in verse 26, and that Jesus, that Messiah, *come in the flesh,* fulfilled this prophecy two thousand years ago.

Dr. Jimmy De Young is a well-known advocate of the dispensationalist-futurist interpretation. Promoted by his fellow Christian Zionists as a prophecy expert, De Young is devoted to convincing evangelicals that the Israelis are about to rebuild the temple destroyed by Titus in 70 AD. Building on the idea that Israel rejected Jesus, he would have us believe that God owes today's Pharisees a chance to complete the said-to-be seven years remaining in the Old Covenant dispensation.

According to De Young this rebuilt temple will be ready for animal sacrifice just before or shortly following "the rapture." The animals, in this case, are said to be a type of perfect red heifer originating with a breeder in Mississippi. The Israelis, it seems, are going to get right with God by sacrificing these red heifers. That's right; those who deny Jesus as the Messiah and final sacrifice are going to sacrifice animals. But alas, they are interrupted when their temple is desecrated by this evil dictator "the Anti-Christ."

You see, it isn't the Israelis who are anti-Christ; it is someone who interrupts when they sacrifice animals. De Young, a defacto lobbyist for the Israeli government, does not consider his interpretation of Daniel 9:27 as less than honest. Neither, of course, do those he would have us continue supporting as the prime beneficiary of our nation's foreign aid budget and Middle Eastern foreign policy.

The idea that anyone would have a future need to sacrifice animals is an insult to Jesus, the perfect and final sacrifice in God's plan. By fulfilling each and every one of one hundred and more Messianic prophecies, Jesus proved he was *the Christ,* that he was Messiah *come in the flesh* (1 John 4:3; 2 John v. 7). No one needs to complete anything by restoring Old Covenant-type temple sacrifices. The only thing this would "complete" is a Pharisaical disregard for His shed blood.

Daniel 9:27 says nothing of a rebuilt temple. There is no temple in this text beyond that which Titus destroyed in 70 AD. Neither is there anyone referred to as "the Anti-Christ,"

> There is no second chance, no seven years remaining in the Old Covenant dispensation.

and/or who makes a covenant allowing the Israelis to sacrifice animals. There is not one verse in Scripture describing a need to sacrifice animals beyond Calvary. As Jesus said before dying that day, *it is finished* (John 19:30). Thus was the seventieth week *finished,* complete, two thousand years ago. There is no second chance, no seven years remaining in the Old Covenant dispensation.

The *Scofield Reference Bible* was released in 1909. In it was the King James Version with interpretational footnotes, the first of their kind to appear in a Bible. But C. I. Scofield did not invent the dispensationalist-futurist interpretation. He merely codified what had previously existed in a loose, unorganized form. Futurists will claim that Scofield's interpretations were not learned from John Nelson Darby only, that they are also traceable to certain second-century church leaders. While this is partially true, it does not mean their interpretations were correct. These men were not divinely inspired. Neither, of course, were the Protestant Reformers, but they did have a completed New Testament canon from which to work. Second- and third-century church leaders did not have this advantage.

Many of Scofield's interpretational notes, especially on end-time events, contradict positions taken by the best Protestant theologians before him. But even Scofield did not identify the aforementioned *he* as do today's dispensationalists. The 1917 revised edition of his reference Bible states: "The *he* of verse 27 is the *prince that shall come* of verse 26, whose people (Rome) destroyed the temple AD 70." This does not agree with today's dispensationalists, the majority of whom (because it is what they are taught) perceive *he* as someone yet to be. Scofield's teaching on Daniel's seventieth week was not fully evolved dispensationalism; it merely laid the groundwork for that which would come.

When Scofield died in 1921, the dispensationalist-futurist interpretation continued to evolve. This accelerated in 1948 when the United Nations officially recognized the Talmudic Zionist state as "Israel." To better fit this masquerade, certain dispensational leaders took the liberty of revising and updating Scofield's original notes. One of the many examples of this is a subtitle added to verses 13-18 of chapter 4 in 1 Thessalonians. It reads: *The Revelation of the Rapture of the Church.* This was added to bolster the idea of a Jesus who descends from but returns to heaven for seven years. Scofield taught this, but had neglected to call it, "the rapture" (see 1917 edition).

Neither, in his notes on Daniel's seventieth-week prophecy, did he identify anyone as "the Anti-Christ." His term for this idea was "Beast" (p. 919, 1917 edition), an entity said to be one and the same with *the Beast* of Revelation (13:4-6) and *the man of sin* (2 Thessalonians 2:3-4). While each of these, whether perceived as a one-man entity or not, would be anti-Christ, it does not identify them as "the Anti-Christ," a term not in the text of the King James translation. This will be explained in the next chapter.

CHAPTER 12

BEFORE OR AFTER TRIBULATION?

Those who read their go-to-heaven idea into 1 Thessalonians 4:13-18 and 1 Corinthians 15 teach this will occur before a seven-year period said to be "the Great Tribulation." This is why they substitute "rapture" for resurrection. By calling it another name it is easier to promote the idea of something which happens before the first resurrection. This is also why dispensationalists futurize and compress sixteen chapters (4-19) in the book of Revelation into their seven-year interpretation. They say these chapters are not mostly history; that the tribulation described therein is future only, and will not commence until after "the rapture." That this is patently false and why they change the theme in 1 Thessalonians 4:13-18 and 1 Corinthians 15 from resurrection to "rapture" is revealed in John's timing of this event:

> And I saw thrones, and they sat upon them, and judgment was given unto them: and I saw the souls of them that were beheaded for the witness of Jesus, and for the word of God, and which had not worshiped the beast, neither his image, neither had received his mark upon their foreheads, or in their

hands; and they lived and reigned with Christ a thousand years. But the rest of the dead lived not again until the thousand years were finished. This is *the first resurrection.*

Revelation 20:4-5 (emphasis mine)

Note how John times *the first resurrection.* It occurs after what dispensationalists call "the Great Tribulation." Also, why does John call this *the first resurrection* if, according to dispensationalists, that in 1 Thessalonians and 1 Corinthians occurs seven years prior? Was John confused? Or, is someone trying to backdate what occurs in 1 Thessalonians and 1 Corinthians by calling it "the rapture"? In light of the fact that it often requires additional errors to cover the first, consider the following claims made by the Judeo-Christian dispensational establishment:

- That Daniel's seventieth week and God's theocratic program (the gospel of the kingdom) was put on hold in AD 34 and until "the rapture" because they say, "Israel rejected Jesus."
- That the Thessalonian and Corinthian churches were comprised of Canaanites, Edomites, and/or other non-Israelites, and for whom God has another program because they say, "Israel rejected Jesus."
- That *the dead in Christ* among Christendom "go to heaven," and "in the rapture," and that this is so because someone else will inherit the kingdom, because they say, "Israel rejected Jesus."
- That a historically non-Christian people (the dead in Phariseeism) are blessed and holy, take part in the first resurrection, and therefore inherit the kingdom of God with Jesus. And, that this is so because today's Pharisees are God's chosen people, because, say the professors, "Israel rejected Jesus two thousand years ago."

- That, when Jesus descends from heaven as per 1 Thessalonians 4:16 it is momentarily only; that he will go back to heaven for a time said to be Daniel's seventieth week (seven years). They say this will happen, "Because Israel rejected Jesus" and is therefore owed a second chance.
- That a nation of neo-Pharisees, Talmudists, and anti-Christs act upon this said-to-be second chance and convert en masse to Christianity—just before Jesus descends from heaven again—a third time!

Incredibly, this is Judeo-Christian eschatology, a chain of errors which evolved out of a need to cover the first, their claim that "Israel rejected Jesus."

God's Litmus Test for Anti-Christs

Evangelical Christians would do well to question an inter-pretation called "the Anti-Christ" and consider this word in its original context. John's, the only application of *anti-Christ* in Scripture, identifies as follows:

> Little children, it is the last time; as ye have heard that *anti-Christ* shall come, even now are there many *anti-Christs;* whereby we know that it is the last time. They went out from us, but they were not of us; for if they had been of us, they would have no doubt continued with us; but they went out, that they might be made manifest that they were not all of us.... Who is a liar but he that denieth that Jesus is the Christ (Messiah)? He is *anti-Christ,* that denieth the Father and the Son, Whosoever denieth the Son (Messiah) the same hath not the Father.
>
> 1 John 2:18-19; 22-23
> (emphasis, parentheses mine)

Beloved, believe not every spirit, but try the spirits whether they are of God; because many false prophets are gone out into the world. Hereby know ye the spirit of God; Every spirit that confesseth that Jesus Christ (Messiah) is come in the flesh is of God. And every spirit that confesseth not that Jesus Christ (Messiah) is come in the flesh is not of God; and this is that spirit of *anti-Christ*, whereof ye have heard that it should come; and even now already is it in the world.

1 John 4:1-3 (parentheses, emphasis mine)

For many deceivers are entered into the world, who confess not that Jesus Christ (Messiah) is come in the flesh. This is a deceiver and *an anti-Christ*.... Whosoever transgresseth, and abideth not in the doctrine of Christ (Messiah) hath not God. He that abideth in the doctrine of Christ (Messiah), he hath both the Father and the Son (Messiah). If there come any unto you, and bring not this doctrine, receive him not into your house, neither bid him Godspeed; for he that biddeth him Godspeed is partaker of his evil deeds.

2 John vv. 7, 9-11 (emphasis, parentheses mine)

You have now read the entire context of *anti-Christ* as used in the King James Version of the Bible. What you found is a theological litmus test—God's litmus test for the *anti-Christ*. In reading all five applications of this word you did not find the one used by Tim LaHaye and Jerry Jenkins (the *Left Behind* series); Hal Lindsey (*The Late, Great Planet Earth*, chapters 19-20); John Hagee (*Jerusalem Countdown*, chapter 13); and others of the Judeo-Christian dispensational establishment. You did not find a future dictator, this supernatural political leader who dispensationalists say will be recognized as "the Anti-Christ" when he breaks a covenant with and attacks the Israelis. What you did find is that Scripture identifies the anti-Christ:

- Present in tense.
- As a plurality.

- In a theological context, one which includes most Israelis.

Any person who denies that Jesus is the Christ, the Messiah of Bible prophecy is, according to these verses, *a liar* and *anti-Christ.* There are no exceptions. Anyone who denies this truth, that Jesus is the Christ, that Messiah is come—*in the flesh,* is, according to Bible definition, *a liar, deceiver,* and *an anti-Christ.* Collectively they are the anti-Christ and are among those for whom Christians are to maintain a policy of nonsupport. We are warned not to receive them into our house, nor to bid them Godspeed lest we be partakers of their evil deeds (2 John vv. 10-11).

Over the years this writer, when presented the opportunity, would ask evangelical Christians the following questions:

1. How do you relate to the word anti-Christ as used in the Bible?
2. Where, in the Bible does the word anti-Christ occur?
3. In what context does Scripture identify the anti-Christ?

Their answer to question #1 was, in the vast majority of cases, in terms of a future and one-man-only entity. When reminded that the question was, "as used in the Bible," they would be confused, having no idea why they were wrong.

About 50 percent could not answer question #2; they could not locate book, chapter, or verse where this word actually occurs. Of the remaining 50 percent, most thought it occurs in the book of Revelation. About half of these also thought it occurs in Daniel's seventieth-week prophecy and/or 2 Thessalonians 2:3-4. A small percentage only knew it was exclusive to John's epistles.

The vast majority responded to question #3 by repeating this word as a proper noun, by using it as the title of a future dictator thought to be "the Anti-Christ." When explained that this is out of context, that *anti-Christ* in context identifies a plurality, and by their theology, they remained confused. They were focused, so focused on the idea of someone who attacks the Israelis that they could not identify the anti-Christ based upon the only application of this word in Scripture. They were oblivious to those who deny that Jesus is the Christ, those who deny and confess not that Messiah—*is come in the flesh.*

Crosstalk is a nationwide Christian radio call-in program and is broadcast by the aforementioned VCY America network. This writer has yet to hear a guest on this program who was not a dispensationalist, who did not agree with the futurist one-man interpretation of *anti-Christ* promoted by "Israel-rejected-Jesus" type teachers. Listening one day as a guest and the host were using this word to focus attention on the idea of a future dictator, I became the next caller. I had told the screener that I, too, wanted to comment regarding the anti-Christ. But while attempting to explain that John's application of this word does not identify this subject in a political and/or in a future one-man context, suddenly, I was cut off. The host then quickly went to the next caller.

A call or two later someone referred to me. This person also, when attempting to explain *anti-Christ* in context, was immediately cut off. This was the result of a program host whose theological training taught him to identify Israel based upon a mantra, the idea that "Israel rejected Jesus." Because he could not reconcile his perception of Israel with *anti-Christ* in context he was unwilling to discuss John's application of this word.

Not until evangelicals are willing to question the teaching that Israel rejected Jesus are they willing to question another error, one designed to cover the first. When they question the idea of a future dictator, those with the Berean spirit first recognize that *anti-Christ,* in context, identifies most Israelis, that their prime minister also is *an anti-Christ*

(2 John v. 7), and as such, we are not to receive him into our house, neither bid him Godspeed (2 John vv. 10-11). Despite this admonition and that in 1 Corinthians 16:22 *(If any man love not the Lord Jesus Christ, let him be Anathema)* the Israeli leader is received into our house (the White House) more often and with more respect than other foreign leaders. When he leaves, our president and representatives, for fear of the Israeli lobby, bid him Godspeed with $10 billion annually in grants, foreign aid, and congressional earmarks, this and more, as Christians focus attention on that future dictator—a smokescreen called "the Anti-Christ."

CHAPTER 13

THE ANCESTRY OF TODAY'S PHARISEES

S hlomo Sand is an Israeli citizen and very educated. He teaches contemporary history at the University of Tel Aviv. In 2008 Professor Sand released his book, *The Invention of the Jewish People.*[9] Extensively footnoted, and with an index of references in the hundreds, Sand documents the ancestry of his fellow Israelis. His conclusion: Most have little Israelitish ancestry, but are descended from an east European (Ashkenazi) people, who in turn, are descended from the ancient Khazar tribes, a people of Turkish origin. Sand's research reveals how large numbers of Khazar/ Ashkenazim migrated to Eastern Europe in the Middle Ages. Driven from the east by Mongol hordes, they arrived as "Jews" and became known as "Jews," having centuries earlier adopted the Talmudic traditions of the Judean Pharisees.

The Ashkenazim, in other words, are not Israelites, are not descended from the Judah portion of Israel. They are mere

---

[9] Shlomo Sand, *The Invention of the Jewish People* (New York and London: Verso Books, 2008).

proselytes to the Talmudic traditions. Remember what Jesus said regarding the Pharisees and their proselytes:

> Woe unto you, scribes and Pharisees, hypocrites! For ye compass sea and land to make one proselyte, and when he is made, ye make him twofold more the child of hell than yourselves.   Matthew 23:15

The dispersion of the Judean Pharisees and their loyalists began in AD 70 with the destruction and ransacking of their temple and capital city. It was after this time, and when significant numbers of them resided in Babylon, that their oral traditions, that their anti-Christ/anti-Christian views, were recorded in a written form called the Talmud. In his forward to *The Babylonian Talmud*, Chief Rabbi Joseph Hertz stated: "The Babylonian Talmud assumed final codified form in the year 500 after the Christian era." According to *The Universal Jewish Encyclopedia*, Vol. VIII, p. 474, 1942 edition:

> The Jewish religion as it is today traces its descent without a break, through all the centuries, from the Pharisees. Their leading ideas and methods found expression in a literature of enormous extent, of which a very great deal is still in existence. The Talmud is the largest and most important single member of that literature.

It does not require much investigating of Talmudism to understand why a proselyte to it is *twofold more the child of hell* than the Pharisees who wrote it. In light of this the term "Judeo-Christian" is an oxymoron, a deceptive term. The teachings of Jesus have nothing in common with today's Pharisees and their Talmud.

That the Ashkenazim, that today's Pharisees, are not descended from the Judah portion of Israel, but are mere proselytes to the religion of the ancient Pharisees, is admitted by many of their historians. The following example is from a chapter titled, "Identity Crisis, A Brief History of the Terms for 'Jew'":

Strictly speaking, it is incorrect to call an ancient Israelite a "Jew" or to call a contemporary Jew an "Israelite" or a "Hebrew" (*The Jewish Almanac*, 1980 edition, p. 3).

The Thirteenth Tribe

Also uncovering their non-Israelitish Khazar ancestry was Arthur Koestler. Listed among the intellectuals in *Who Is Who In World Jewry,* Koestler has a long list of honors and titles originating in Europe and in America. In 1976 he published *The Thirteenth Tribe,* a book in which he thoroughly documented the Ashkenazi/Khazar origins of most Israelis. He explains how Israelis of Ashkenazim or east European ancestry are descended, primarily, from the ancient Khazars, a people who migrated to eastern Europe from Asia beginning about a thousand years ago.

As Koestler documents, they arrived as "Jews," but were proselytes only, having converted in the seventh century. He describes in great detail their conversion as beginning about the year 740 AD and as an edict by their leader King Bulan, who mandated "Judaism" as the state religion. In his chapter on Race and Myth, Koestler states: "The finding of physical anthropology shows that, contrary to popular view, there is no Jewish race." What Koestler and other historians concede is that "Jewish" (in the vernacular) identifies not the descendants of the Judean Pharisees, but their proselytes, the followers of Talmudism. This is especially true in light of the fact that "Jew" as the name of Israel's religion became obsolete as it was replaced by "Christian," by Israel's prophesied new name. This was explained in chapter 4. Koestler, in explaining the origins of the Ashkenazim states:

> Their ancestors came not from the Jordan but from the Volga, not from Canaan, but from the Caucasus... and that genetically they are more related to the Hun,

Uigur, and Magyar tribes than to the seed of Abraham, Isaac, and Jacob.[10]

Ashkenazi-Khazar People Not of Judah

Preceding Arthur Koestler's research on this subject was that of Nathan M. Pollock, professor of Medieval Jewish History at Tel Aviv University. Pollock, after forty years of research, concluded that most Israelis, being of Ashkenazim and therefore Khazar ancestry, are not real Jews but proselytes only. They are not, therefore, descended from the Judah portion of Israel, and even if they were, would not be representative of the entire twelve tribes of Israel. And, what about "Ashkenazim," what is the origin of this term?

In the tenth chapter of the book of Genesis is listed the sons of Noah's three sons.

> Now these are the generations of the sons of Noah, Shem, Ham, and Japheth: and unto them were sons born after the flood. The sons of Japheth; Gomer, and Magog, and Madai, and Javan, and Tubal, and Meshech, and Tiras. And the sons of Gomer; *Ashkenaz,* and Rijphath, and Togarmah. And the sons of Javan; Elishah, and Tarshish, Kittim, and Dodanim. By these were the isles of the Gentiles (nations) divided in their lands; every one after his tongue, after their families, in their nations.
>
> Genesis 10:1-5 (emphasis, parenthesis mine)

Note how Ashkenaz is a son, not of Shem, but of Japheth. Does this explain why historians among the Ashkenazim admit they are of non-Israelitish ancestry? Is there is a link between Japheth and Ashkenazim-Khazar people? More research needs to be done on this subject.

---

[10] Arthur Koestler, *The Thirteenth Tribe* (New York, NY: Random House, 1976), 17.

Also of significance is that the term *Semite*, which derives from Shem and includes the ancient Assyrians, Babylonians, Carthaginians, Ethiopian, Phoenician, and other ancient people of the Middle East. "Semitic" therefore is not specific of Israelites only. It is a broadly defined word, one which, if inclusive of today's Pharisees, does not give them an exclusive right to.

Johns Hopkins DNA Study Adds to Evidence

A DNA study released late in 2012 confirms what Jewish historians have documented in the previously mentioned books. Geneticist Dr. Eran Elhaik (Jewish) of the Johns Hopkins School of Public Health, and in a study involving Ashkenazi European Jews, has confirmed that their dominant genetic makeup originates among the people of ancient Khazaria. Elhaik's research found little support for the Rhineland Hypothesis, the theory that modern Jews descend from Israelites who fled Palestine after the Muslim conquest in 638 AD.

His study agrees with research done in 2001 by fellow Jewish geneticist Dr. Ariella Oppenheim of Hebrew University. Oppenheim, likewise, found that Jewish DNA supports the Khazarian, not the Rhineland Hypothesis. Both studies, therefore, support what has been documented in other ways. They prove that the genome of European "Jews" is a mixture of ancient peoples, many of whom were not Israelites. These studies are easily accessed by doing a Web search for: *Genome Evolution of Jewish Population Johns Hopkins.*

There is much more available on the non-Israelitish Khazar ancestry of the Ashkenazim, most of which is by their own historians. Not surprisingly, the Zionist element among them, when they cannot give these historians and their research the silent treatment, dismiss them as, "anti-Semitic." Also giving this subject the silent treatment are seminary, Bible college professors, and evangelical leaders. They repeat on a daily basis their opening line. They tell us that, "Because Israel rejected Jesus," God's promise in Genesis 12:3 *(I will bless them that bless thee, and curse him that curseth thee)* applies to today's Pharisees. But, they conveniently ignore the non-Israelitish Khazar ancestry of those for whom they promote support, those whom they call "Israel."

Other Non-Israelitish "Jews"

Airlifted to the Israeli state in the 1980s and 1990s were "Black Jews of Ethiopia." Their features, being typical of North African people, are totally different than Israelis of Ashkenazim-Khazar descent. Despite this difference it is claimed that both groups, white and black, are of Israelitish ancestry and therefore "Jewish." Also of color and claimed as descendants of Jacob-Israel are "Jews" of India, China, Yemen, Iran, Egypt, and Spain. All these groups have features similar to the majority population in their respective countries. This means they are different in ancestry, their commonality lying in religion only. Portions of these groups have found their way to the Israeli state where they now reside as a racial minority in a population dominated by those of Ashkenazim-Khazar descent.

The inclusion of non-Ashkenazi, non-Khazar groups into the Israeli state is based, it seems, on the idea they are descendants of a still lost Ten Tribes of Israel. Thus is the theme of a calendar distributed by Jewish Voice Ministries International of Phoenix, Arizona. Pictured above each month in their 2013 calendar are members of the Gefat Tribe (Ethiopia), the Hmar and Mizo communities (Manipur, India), the Lemba Tribe (Zimbabwe), and numerous others not of Ashkenazim-Khazar descent.

In listening to the *Jewish Voice* TV program and examining their *Jewish Voice Today* magazine, one gets the impression that it is anyone but a historically Christian people who are Israelites. Judeo-Christian leaders tend to agree with this.

Only when Israel is identified correctly as one and the same with historic Christianity do they object.

In 1995 this writer received an interesting envelope. From author Yair Davidy in Susia, Israel, it contained a flyer promoting his newly published book, *The Tribes*. Unlike Jewish Voice Ministries, Davidy's book does not promote the Gefat, Lemba, and other African, etc., people as descendants of Jacob-Israel. Davidy, in a 498-page book with maps and illustrations, and citing Biblical, archaeological, and other evidence, states unequivocally that the non-Jew ten-tribed portion of Israel migrated north and west to Europe. His research concludes that the Anglo-Saxon, Celtic, Germanic, Scandinavian, and related European people are descended from these ancient Israelites. Yair Davidy is not the only Israeli and/or Jewish researcher to reveal this truth. In 1953 Dr. Alfred Lilienthal, in his book, *What Price Israel?*, makes the following statement.

> Here's a paradox, a paradox, a most ingenious paradox: an anthropological fact, many Christians (Europeans) may have much more Hebrew-Israelite blood in their veins than most of their Jewish neighbors.[11]

Speaking before the Cornell Club of Washington on September 10, 1985, Dr. Lilienthal declared the following:

> Many (contemporary Jews) of whom have clamored to go back (to Palestine) never had antecedents (ancestors) in that part of the world. Many (Christian/Europeans) who do not want to go back have had a better claim. Queen Victoria (England) herself belonged to an Israelite society that traced its membership back to the Ten Lost Tribes of Israel.[12]

---

[11] Dr. Alfred M. Lilienthal, *What Price Israel?* (Chicago, Illinois: Henry Regnery Company, 1953), 223.

[12] Dr. Alfred M. Lilienthal, "Middle East Terror—The Double Standard: Address" (Washington, DC: The 30th Anniversary Fund, Phi Beta Kappa Association, 1985), 5.

These are but a few of many well-researched authoritative writings confirming the mostly non-Israelitish origins of Israelis and contemporary Jews. The authors are Jewish and honestly motivated, but because their writings are not subservient to Zionist ambitions they receive the silent treatment by evangelical leaders. In thousands of hours and years of listening to Christian radio and TV this writer has yet to hear a Judeo-Christian leader address the Ashkenazim-Khazar factor. They continually remind us that "Israel rejected Jesus," a statement fitting most Ashkenazim-Khazar people, but they do not tell us the rest of the story.

CHAPTER 14

ISRAELITES THE NUCLEUS OF THE CHURCH

The Gospels and the book of Acts identify the first Christians as the *thousands of Jews* who accepted Jesus and the New Covenant. Then, after the gospel was preached *to the Jew first,* it was taken to a greater number of Israelites, those of the dispersion. Having been divorced by God and *scattered abroad* centuries earlier they were now north and west of Palestine, in the Mediterranean area and further, well into Europe. This explains why maps in the rear of most Bibles show Christianity as spreading, primarily, north and west of Palestine, in a European direction.

Thus was Jesus and the New Covenant accepted, by *the Jew first,* then *the Greek,* the Greek-speaking, and other non-Jew Israelites of the dispersion. Thus also were Judah and Israel, after centuries of separation, united. They were now *both one* (Ephesians 2:14) in Christ Jesus. United in One they were becoming known as *Christians,* the God-ordained *new name* for Israelites and their religion. The Bible narrative then ends in the latter part of the first century, with a church comprised of Israelites.

Because it contradicts their basis for identifying Israel, seminary-trained ministers will, but do not like to admit, that it was Israelites, that it was *thousands of Jews* who were the first Christians. They will admit that the church began as an Israelitish institution; however, they are quick to say it did not remain so. They tell us this occurred as the descendants of those *thousands of Jews* intermarried with and were absorbed by a greater number of non-Israelite Christians. They do not identify the ancestry of these said-to-be non-Israelites.

Whether they were Edomites, Canaanites, Hittites, or others, they do not say; only that they were Gentiles and therefore non-Israelites. This type of dogmatism is the result of a seminary student who was taught, and who naively accepted, the idea that all Israelites were Jews. Then, and because he reads in the New Testament epistles of *Gentiles* in contradistinction to *Jews,* he builds another error upon the first. With no contextual evidence, and/or with contextual evidence to the contrary, he erroneously assumes that Christians called *Gentiles* in the New Testament epistles were not Israelites.

> This was Israelites marrying Israelites, marrying after their kind.

Israelitish from the beginning, the church did not then become otherwise as *thousands of Jews* and their descendants intermarried with Christians called *Gentiles* (the Diaspora). This was Israelites marrying Israelites, marrying after their kind. They were not as the mixed marriage which occurred when Esau took to wife Judith the Hittite, that which caused *a grief of mind* (Genesis 26:35) unto his parents Isaac and Rebekah.

These Christian Israelites knew that *sin is the transgression of the law* (1 John 3:4), that *the law of the Lord* (Deuteronomy 7:3-6, etc.) forbade mixed marriages. This is clearly explained in Ezra (chapter 10) and Nehemiah (13:23-30). Dispensational teaching, to the contrary, these Scriptures are among those which are *profitable for doctrine, for reproof, for correction, for instruction in righteousness* (2 Tim. 3:16). What was condemned as sin by Ezra and Nehemiah was written in these books for our learning and understanding that we not repeat these mistakes.

From the Mediterranean Area to Europe

Christendom, as defined in *Webster's New Collegiate Dictionary*, is: "Christianity; the part of the world in which Christianity prevails." Now, in which part of the world does Christianity prevail? Currently, America is the nation where Christianity is the most prevalent. There are more churches per capita and Christian-related organizations in the USA than any nation on earth. Others, those such as India and China are larger in population but do not have a Christian history as does America.

It would be safe to say that more Bibles and Christian teaching material originate in America than in the rest of the world combined. But it was not always this way. The Puritans, the Christians who founded this nation, came from Europe. Christendom for centuries was one and the same with the people of Europe. It was to Europe that the oracles of God, that the Christian religion, came with a people from the Mediterranean area. This was not by coincidence. There is a reason why Christianity spread primarily in a European direction. It was following the migrations of Israel, *the twelve tribes scattered abroad* (James 1:1).

Many scholarly books have been written on this subject. Containing historical, archaeological, and anthropological evidence they document the Israelitish origins of people called Scythians, Cimmerians, and others. Having migrated from the south and east these people became the Germanic tribes, those who later broke up and formed the Angles, Saxons, Celts, Jutes, Danes, and Vikings.

Other Germanic tribes, those who migrated more south and west, became the Gothic nations, the Lombards, Franks, Vandals, Burgundians, and others. These were the nations of people who, in the first centuries of the New Covenant era, abandoned pagan religions to become, as the dictionary defines Christendom, "The part of the world in which Christianity prevails." This was the result of the New Covenant, that which was made two thousand years ago with *the house of Israel and with the house of Judah,* the twelve tribes which were *scattered abroad* at that time.

Israel, the Custodian of Christianity

By the end of the ninth century Christianity dominated among Europeans. Not all Diaspora Israelites were religious, but among those who were, Christianity dominated. This was not true of non-European people at that time, nor is it today.

Those who identify Israel by stating, "Israel rejected Jesus," have always been at a loss to explain why Christianity is not then evenly distributed among the other *families of the earth.* Why is the new Christian covenant, that which was promised to Israel and Judah and instituted by Jesus, so disproportionately found among people of European descent? Why is it not found, proportionately, among the people of Asia and Africa? Why did the apostle Paul, a missionary *to the Gentiles* (the Diaspora), not travel south into Africa, or east into Asia, into India and China? The best explanation for this is that the Diaspora, *far off, through all the countries whither thou hast driven them* (Dan. 9:7) were not in the Far East or deepest Africa. They were in the Mediterranean area and *far off* into Europe.

Because it was *Israelites: to whom pertaineth* and to whom *were committed the oracles of God;* it was they who completed that Book by adding to it the Gospels, the book of Acts, the epistles, and Revelation. Written in Greek, the New Testament canon, when first translated, was available primarily in Latin and to the clergy only, not to the masses. The earliest non-Latin versions, in the Anglo-Saxon dialects, appeared in the seventh and eighth centuries. But it was the Wycliffe Version (English) and the Gutenberg printing press in the early and mid-1400s which made *the oracles of God* available to common people in their own language.

This combination triggered a renaissance of invention and discovery, one that brought Europe out of the Middle Ages. Up to and during this time *the oracles of God* were not committed to the other *families of the earth.* Through no fault of their own the indigenous people of Asia, Africa, the Pacific Islands, and the Americas were not included in the call of Abraham. This is why the Bible and the Christian religion are not woven into their culture as it is with Europeans. Again, we must be reminded that it was not the other *families of the earth,* but *Israelites: to whom pertaineth...; and of whom as concerning the flesh Christ came* (Rom. 9:4-5).

From Europe to America

Abraham was told by Yahweh that He would be *a God unto thee, and unto thy seed after thee.* If we believe Jesus is God this prophecy makes sense only if the descendants of Jacob-Israel are a people for whom Jesus is God. This is true among Christians only. Israel therefore would have to be, historically, a Christian people, which Europeans only are. Also promised of Abraham was that he would be *a father of many nations* and that he and Sarah's descendants would number as *the stars of the sky* and *the dust of the earth.* Isaac's wife Rebekah was told she would be *the mother of thousands of millions* (Genesis 24:60).

Again, these are prophecies which fit the *many nations* of Europe and certain nations outside of Europe, the US, Canada, Australia, and New Zealand, etc. (those predominately Christian because they were founded by Europeans). That Israel in the latter days would be a vast multitude a people *of many nations* is a prophecy which does not fit today's Pharisees, one of the world's smaller ethnic groups.

Israel, numbering in the hundreds of thousands of people, outgrew Palestine first. Then after centuries of multiplying were in the millions and outgrew even Europe. But God had a plan. Reserved for His Israel covenant people was a far-off land, the New World. Twenty-five centuries previous, while the covenant people were still in Palestine, God had told King David:

> Moreover, I will appoint a place for my people Israel, and will plant them, that they may dwell in a place of their own, and move no more; neither shall the children of wickedness afflict them any more, as before time. 2 Samuel 7:10

America must be that appointed place, a place for God's Israel covenant people. It was here in the wilderness of America, in a land between two seas, that Christian Israel would be safe from the Assyrian and Babylonian armies. It was here that Mongol and Islamic "hordes" could not reach Israel as they had in Europe. It was here also that Christian Israelites would be protected from the Roman papal system and its inquisitions. A holocaust which took the lives of millions of Christian Israelites, the Inquisition,[13] is little spoken of today.

Our nation's Puritan Pilgrim founders were Christian Israelites who, knowing God's promises, called this land across the sea "The Wilderness," the "New Canaanland," and other Biblical terms.[14] As they left Europe for America they said their purpose was to establish "the Kingdom of God."

Israel's last and greatest migration began when a ship called the Mayflower left Europe for America. Between 1620 and

---

[13] Read *Foxe's Book of Martyrs* by John Foxe.

[14] Peter Marshall and David Manuel, *The Light and the Glory* (Old Tappan, NJ: Fleming H. Revell Co., 1977).

1900 occurred the largest mass migration in human history as Christian Israelites, by the tens of millions, sailed west across the mighty Atlantic. Arriving in America they founded what would become, not only a Christian

> Israel's last and greatest migration began when a ship called the Mayflower left Europe for America.

nation, but the greatest nation ever known. It is here, after centuries of westward migration, that the Covenant People will move no more.

We are, in all probability, the recipients of *the kingdom of God,* that which Jesus said would be *taken from you* (Judea/old Jerusalem) *and given to a nation bringing forth the fruits thereof* (Matt. 21:43). America, more than any other, is *a nation bringing forth the fruits thereof.* The exact opposite is true regarding the self-named state of "Israel," a nation of people who pattern their religion after the Judean Pharisees, those whom *the kingdom of God* was taken from.

For over a century now it has been America, primarily, from which the light of God's Word has gone to the ends of the earth. Only in America are there millions of Christian Israelites who distribute more Bibles to the rest of the world than other nations combined. The largest Bible publishing houses, once in England, are now in America. This is not mere coincidence; it is what Israel was prophesied to do.

Also in America, and in fulfillment of prophecy, are vast agricultural lands, forests, water and mineral resources, and a suitable climate. Our free enterprise economic system, that which rose out of our religion, has given us the incentive for inventions and discoveries which are the envy of the world. We have been blessed far beyond any nation on earth. It was in recognition of this that our annual Thanksgiving holiday was established.

> Arise, shine; for thy light is come, and the glory of the Lord is risen upon thee. For, behold, the darkness shall cover the earth, and gross darkness the people: but the Lord shall arise upon thee, and his glory shall be seen upon thee.   Isaiah 60:1-2

The glory of the Lord, the glory of Jesus Christ, has risen upon America like no other nation on earth. North America is *Hephzibah and Beulah land* (Isaiah 62:4), that beautiful *(Beulah)* land of which we sing ("America the Beautiful"). No, the Bible does not mention America by name, but it has much to say about a latter-day people and nation called the *Stone Kingdom.* Raised up, by God, for special service to the world, this Stone Kingdom would become the world's dominant nation and would be in existence at the second coming of Jesus the Messiah.

That the USA was described in Bible prophecy was recognized by one Reverend F. E. Pitts of Nashville, Tennessee. As recorded in the Congressional Record of 1857, he spoke the following words in an address to congress:

> There are many passages in scripture which are universally admitted, by the very learned and judicious, to foretell the rise of a great nationality in the latter times. These predictions cannot, by any reasonable construction, be applied to the rise of such nationality in the land of Judea; but are most wonderfully descriptive of this United States of America, and of no other country under heaven.

Reverend Pitts knew that Isaiah's and other prophecies could not apply to a non-Christian people or to the site of ancient Judea, a small, semi-arid parcel of land in old Palestine.

The Spirit of God to Be upon Israel

> Yet now hear, O Jacob my servant; and Israel, whom I have chosen: Thus saith the Lord that made thee, and formed thee from the womb, which will help thee;

Fear not, O Jacob, my servant; and thou, Jes-u-run, whom I have chosen. For I will pour water upon him that is thirsty, and floods upon the dry ground: *I will pour my spirit upon thine offspring:* And they shall spring up as among the grass, as willows by the water courses. One shall say, I am the Lord's; and another shall call himself by the name of Jacob; and another shall subscribe with his hand unto the Lord, and surname himself by the name of Israel.

Isaiah 44:1-5 (emphasis mine)

In fulfillment of Isaiah's, Joel's, and other prophecies, God poured His Spirit *upon thine offspring,* upon Jacob's descendants, on the day of Pentecost in AD 33. Because the gospel was preached *to the Jew first,* and because His Spirit, His Word, does not return unto Him void, *thousands of Jews,* believing this message, were becoming known as *Christians,* their *new name.*

After *the Jew* it was preached to the Diaspora, the non-Jew Israelites, called *Gentiles* in the New Testament epistles. The *lost sheep of the house of Israel,* it was they who the apostle Paul was ministering to in his missionary journeys. This is where the Bible narrative ends, at the end of the first century, and with a church, with the New Covenant congregations comprised of Jew and non-Jew Israelites. Now, read Isaiah 59:20-21 again and ask yourself, did the ancestors of these Christian Israelites denounce Jesus for Phariseeism, and if so, when?

And the Redeemer shall come to Zion, and unto them that turn from transgression in Jacob, saith the Lord. As for me, this is my covenant with them, saith the Lord; My spirit that is upon thee, and my words which I have put in thy mouth, shall not depart out of thy mouth, nor out of the mouth of thy seed, nor out of the mouth of thy seed's seed, saith the Lord, from henceforth and forever.   Isaiah 59:20-21

So, *the Redeemer* came to, and His Spirit and His Word remained upon, repentant Israelites. That which He put in their mouth did not depart out of their mouth. Neither would it depart out of the mouth of their seed, nor their *seed's seed...forever.* Isaiah's prophecy tells us that Christianity did not fizzle out among Jacob's descendants. It tells us that Israel, the nucleus of the church, was not supplanted by a mixture of other ethnic groups. Had this been the case it would have been revealed by the Lord God who does *nothing, but he revealeth his secret unto his servants the prophets* (Amos 3:7).

God, who declares *the end from the beginning* (Isaiah 46:10), *by the scriptures of the prophets* (Romans 16:26), says nothing about some other ethnic group supplanting genetic Israel as the nucleus of the church. But He does say that millions of today's descendants of those *thousands of Jews* would be known as Christians, by *another name.* Prophecy also tells us that the hundreds of millions of descendants of non-Jew Diaspora Israelites would also be known as *Christians,* by Israel's *new name.* This explains why Christianity is Eurocentric. This only, explains why Christendom, historically, is one and the same with the Anglo-Saxon, Celtic, Germanic, Scandinavian, and related European people.

We are the descendants of *the house of Israel...and the house of Judah,* those with whom *the new covenant,* the New Testament, was established on that night of the Last Supper two thousand years ago. We are the descendants of those to whom Hebrews, James, and the New Testament epistles were written, the very Scriptures which describe the church as an Israelitish institution. But we do not know who we are. Told that Israel rejected Jesus, we assume, because we are Christian—we are not Israelites.

We recognize, it seems, that Islam prevails among Arabs, that Buddhists and Hindus are of Asia, that Shinto is Japanese, Confucian Chinese, and that other non-Christian religions prevail primarily outside of Europe. But we, the Anglo-Saxon, Celtic, Germanic, Scandinavian, and related Europeans, give little or no thought as to why Christianity is Eurocentric. We will admit that every major Bible translation, that every great Bible expositor and Christian movement in memory, has originated among us, but we dismiss this as mere coincidence because everybody knows, "Israel rejected Jesus." So focused we are on that opening line we cannot see the forest for the trees.

There are pockets of individuals among other ethnic groups, among other *families of the earth,* who profess Christianity, but this has occurred only in the last two hundred years or so, and—only as Europeans introduce them to the Book. It is never the other way around. Neither, to the extent that Christianity exists among other *families of the earth* has it proved to be self-sustaining. Christianity, in its purest form, is found and is self-sustaining only among those:

> Who are Israelites; to whom pertaineth the adoption, and the glory, and the covenants, and the giving of the law, and the service of God, and the promises; Whose are the fathers, and of whom as concerning the flesh Christ came. Romans 9:4-5

Whose, then, *are the fathers, and of whom as concerning the flesh* did Christ come? Was it, as the seminaries teach, the Judean Pharisees and their loyalists only? No, it was all Israelites, *near and far off, through all the countries whither thou hast driven them.* It was *the twelve tribes which are scattered abroad,* those who would become the world's only ethnic group who, historically, are a Christian people. True to Isaiah's prophecy the spirit of Christianity did not depart out of the mouth of Jacob's seed, or out of the mouth of his *seed's seed* (59:21).

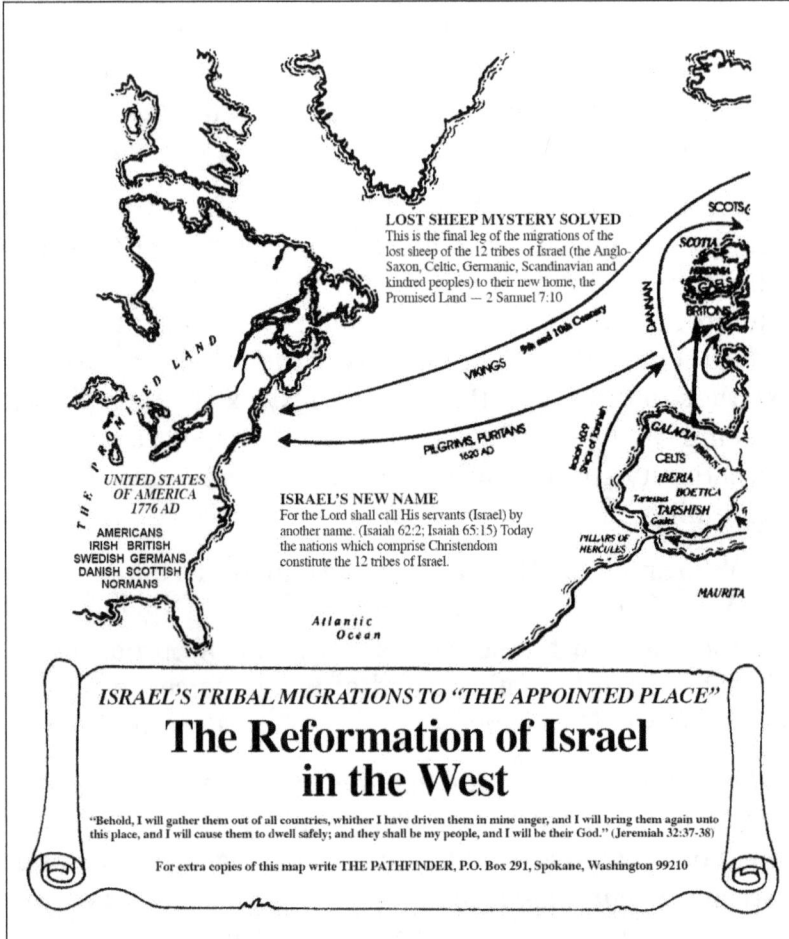

LOST SHEEP MYSTERY SOLVED
This is the final leg of the migrations of the lost sheep of the 12 tribes of Israel (the Anglo-Saxon, Celtic, Germanic, Scandinavian and kindred peoples) to their new home, the Promised Land — 2 Samuel 7:10

ISRAEL'S NEW NAME
For the Lord shall call His servants (Israel) by another name. (Isaiah 62:2; Isaiah 65:15) Today the nations which comprise Christendom constitute the 12 tribes of Israel.

ISRAEL'S TRIBAL MIGRATIONS TO "THE APPOINTED PLACE"

The Reformation of Israel in the West

"Behold, I will gather them out of all countries, whither I have driven them in mine anger, and I will bring them again unto this place, and I will cause them to dwell safely; and they shall be my people, and I will be their God." (Jeremiah 32:37-38)

For extra copies of this map write THE PATHFINDER, P.O. Box 291, Spokane, Washington 99210

THE CAUCASUS MOUNTAINS
Celto-Saxondom (the Israelites) received the
name Caucasian after migrating, passing
through the Caucasus Mountains.

Norwegian
Sea

NORSEMEN 9TH CENTURY

VIKINGS
SWITHOID

SCAN-DIN-AVIA

NORSEMEN

ROSH
900 AD

MESHECH
(MOSCOW MUSCOVY)
Ezekiel 38

MAGOG

TUBAL
(TOBOLSK BULGARIA)

PICTS
CALEDONIA
CYMRI
CIMBRI
JUTES
ANGLI

GOTHS

TEUTONES
SWITHOID

SCYTHIA
SCYTHIANS
SARMATIA

BRIT-AIN
CELTS
ISLES"

SAXONS
SUEONES

ANGLES
GERMANIC TRIBES

WARNI
FRANKS
SACKSEN
SACKI
SACA

BURGUNDI
ALEMANI

DNEIPER R.

GOTHS
GETAE

SCOLOTOI
GAUTHIE

ISKUZA

TOCARMAH

SACAGE

MESAGETAE

SACAE

PICTONES
BRITANNI
BRITONES
OSTROGOTHS
ROMANS

CELTICA
VISIGOTHS

VENETIA

SCYTHIANS

DNIESTER R.

VISTULA R.

CAUCASUS
MTS.

Caspian
Sea

IBERIA

PASSAGE
OF ISRAEL

GALLIA
DAN
100 BC

DANUBE R.

GETAE
300 BC

CALEDONIA

THRACE
MACEDONIA

Rome

Black Sea

BYTHINIA
PONTUS COLCHIS
GALATIA

PONTUS COLCHIS

ASSYRIA

Hara

Halah
Habor

SARMATIA

KIMERIO
THE DISPERSION 1 PETER 1:1
CAPPADOCIA
PHOCEA
DARDANIA

CIMMERI

VOLCI
CRETE

Danite
Phoenicians to
Iberia and Hibernia.
1250 BC

DANA

CYPRUS

Tyre

TIGRIS R.

MEDIA

NIA

Carthage

Mediterranean Sea

BETH-SAK
KHUMRI
Samaria

EUPHRATES R.

Jerusalem
740-721 BC

BABYLON

Jeremiah
with Scota

PERSIA

PHUT

Alexandria

Tophet
588 BC

EGYPT

Cairo

NILE R.

N

**ISRAEL'S CAPTIVITY BEGINS
THE MIGRATION WESTWARD**
From 740-721 BC the 10 tribes plus most of
Judahites taken into captivity (2 Kings 18:9-16)

A Second Chance for Today's Pharisees?

As explained in chapter 11, it is because the seminaries need another error (or lie) to cover the first that they change the theme in 1 Thessalonians 4:13-18 and 1 Corinthians 15:20-58 from that of *the resurrection,* to *inherit the kingdom of God,* to their rapture/go-to-heaven interpretation. First they focus on the Ashkenazim on a nation of neo-Pharisees as Israel. Then, because the deceased (the dead in Phariseeism) among these, historically, non-Christian people will not rise in *the resurrection,* cannot *inherit the kingdom,* and are not therefore Israel, seminary professors read into these texts their rapture/go-to-heaven interpretation.

Needing a second chance for the beneficiaries of their opening line, the professors create a Jesus who descends from heaven the second time but does not then gather non-Christians *out of his kingdom.* Theirs, the Jesus of dispensationalism descends from heaven the second time, but only to return and descend again—a third time! And of course, in between this second and third time is their futurized seventieth week, a convenient second chance for today's Pharisees.

There is no second chance, for neo-Pharisees or anyone else. When Jesus descends from heaven the second—and last— time he will *send forth his angels, and they shall gather out of his kingdom all things that offend, and them which do iniquity* (Matt. 13:41).

What could be more descriptive of *them which do iniquity* and *things which offend* than today's Pharisees and their Federal Reserve debt/usury money system, that which is used to rob and enslave us?[15] And, what could be more offensive to a returning Jesus than their disproportionate representation in, and support for, the abortion and pornography

---

[15] Web search "Federal Reserve Fraud" for suppressed truth on this subject.

industries, homosexual rights organizations, and other *things that offend?* And, how about the decisions they make when representing us as federal and Supreme Court judges? The aforementioned *things that offend* owe their existence to federal and Supreme Court judges, whose decisions give these sins legal protection. This, the "Judeo" ethic, is totally contrary to that of first-century circumcised-in-*the-heart* Jews. These are the ethics of neo-Pharisees, a present day *synagogue of Satan.*

Congress does not have to approve and can even remove openly anti-Christ/anti-Christian federal and Supreme Court judges, but they do not. They dare not, *for fear of* getting bombarded with smears and negative coverage by the mainstream news media. This happens because "Big Media" is mostly owned and/or controlled by the same anti-Christ/anti-Christian element which is disproportionately represented among *things which offend.*

This was alluded to by Nicholas Kristof, columnist for the *New York Times.* He stated: "I can't think of a single evangelical working for a major news-paper organization."[16] The same can be said of federal and Supreme Court judges. Openly anti-Christ people get

> Something is wrong when those who confess that Messiah *is come in the flesh,* are ruled by those who do not.

appointed to, and are approved for the bench, but Bible-believing Christians, it seems, need not apply. There is a total absence of evangelical Christians in high-ranking positions of authority in Washington DC. Something is wrong when Christians, when those who confess that Messiah *is come in the flesh,* are ruled by those who do not. We should not, however, be totally dismayed by the current situation.

---

[16] St. Paul Pioneer Press, March 7, 2003.

For the Lord loveth judgment, and forsaketh not his saints; they are preserved for ever: but the seed of *the wicked* shall be cut off. The righteous shall inherit the land and dwell therein for ever. The mouth of the righteous speaketh wisdom, and his tongue talketh of judgment. The law of his God is in his heart; none of his steps shall slide.... Wait on the Lord and keep his way, and he shall exalt thee to inherit the land: when *the wicked* are cut off thou shalt see it. I have seen *the wicked* in great power, and spreading himself like a green bay tree. Yet he passed away, and, lo, he was not: yea, I sought him, but he could not be found.

Psalm 37:28-31; 34-36 (emphasis mine)

We see today *the wicked in great power, and spreading... like a green bay tree.* In addition to major news outlets and the private "Federal" Reserve banking system, Hollywood also is their domain. In the 1950s they did give us a movie called *The Ten Commandments*, but since it has been mostly PG-, R-, and even X-rated films. When nudity and profanity are not enough they will add to the decadence anti-religious themes. In Hollywood this means anti-Christian, non-Christian religions are tolerated. Other areas where the wicked are *in great power and spreading* are state and local governments, public education, Ivy League universities, and the list goes on, as *Mystery, Babylon the Great* (Revelation 17:5) tightens its stranglehold on America and the world.

One and the same with the wicked are New World Order-type secret societies and "think tanks." The average Christian and voter has never heard of the Trilateral Commission, the Council on Foreign Relations, the Bilderberg group, and others. This, despite the fact that membership in these groups is an important prerequisite for appointment to a presidential cabinet and other high-ranking positions. Which major political party wins the White House makes little difference. The newly elected president, as did his predecessor, will select most of his cabinet from the membership roster of these groups. This is very significant and is known, but is not reported by major news outlets, because they, too, are controlled by members of these groups.

Mainstream news anchors and reporters, often earning huge figures annually, are quite willing to suppress this and other truth in order to maintain their millionaire lifestyle *(for the love of money is the root of all evil)*. These are the prostitutes of journalism, those whose primary application of the word *conspiracy* ("conspiracy theory") would have us believe they exist in theory only. Their complicity proves otherwise.

God does provide the wicked with a second chance; however, it will not occur according to dispensational teaching. It will not occur between some future "rapture" and third coming of Christ. The Biblical second chance is available at this very moment. It is known as *repentance.*

CHAPTER 15

DO NOT HIDE TRUTH
UNDER A BUSHEL

> Ye are the light of the world. A city that is set on a hill cannot be hid. Neither do men light a candle, and put it under a bushel, but on a candlestick; and it giveth light unto all that are in the house. Let your light so shine before men, that they may see your good works, and glorify your Father which is in heaven.
>
> Matthew 5:14-16

Jesus (*the light of the world* [John 8:12]) was speaking to Israelites in his Sermon on the Mount when he told them, *Ye are the salt of the earth...the light of the world.* Not true of all Israelites, this statement was limited to those who would accept Him as Messiah and follow his example. One and the same with the church, it is the deceased among them who are *the dead in Christ,* and who *inherit the kingdom of God* with their Savior when they *rise again in the resurrection, at the last day.* Politically correct it is not, but this event will not include, proportionately, the other *families of the earth,* those who the first Christian (European) missionaries did not reach with God's Word until fairly recent times.

> Who rises in the resurrection proves who Israel is—and who Israel is not.

It is Biblically impossible for those who were born outside of God's covenants, for those who lived and died without written or oral knowledge of Jesus, to be included among *the dead in Christ.* Thus it is that who rises in the resurrection proves who Israel is—and who Israel is not. Remember, it was Israelites *to whom pertaineth,* and of whom Jesus and the New Testament writers promised that Christians among them would *inherit the kingdom of God*—his theocratic plan. This eliminates today's Pharisees and other, historically, non-Christian people.

Who then, *of all the families of the earth,* will prove they are Israel by being disproportionately represented among *the dead in Christ?* There is only one answer to this question. It is the Anglo-Saxon, Celtic, Germanic, Scandinavian, and related European people. They only, *of all the families of the earth* are, historically, a Christian people and are therefore Israel.

> Having identified the millions of descendants of those *"thousands of Jews"* long ago, you have untangled the paradox. You now understand why millions of today's evangelicals wrongly assume that, because they are Christian—they are not Israelites!

Notable Christian Israel Believers

Throughout history many notable believers have known and have taught the Christian Israel truth. The following is a sample:

- Dr. Mordecai F. Ham, Baptist evangelist under whom Dr. Billy Graham was converted.
- Dr. G. Campbell Morgan, known as, "the prince of expositors," Congregationalist.
- Bishop Jonathan Holt Titcomb, Anglican theologian.
- Dr. Dinsdale T. Young, Methodist evangelist.
- Evangelist F. F. Bosworth, Christian Missionary Alliance.
- Henry Ford, 1863-1947, US industrialist.
- Rudyard Kipling, 1865-1936, writer and poet.
- Queen Victoria, 1819-1901, English leader.
- Sir Isaac Newton, 1642-1727, English scientist.
- King Alfred the Great, 849-901, English leader.
- The Venerable Bede, 673(?)-735, theologian and Anglo-Saxon historian.

These Christians believed and taught that the Anglo-Saxon, Celtic, Germanic, Scandinavian, and related European people are descended from ancient Israel. It is worthy of note that Billy Graham, converted under Dr. Mordecai F. Ham, would have known but avoided teaching this truth. Related or not, Graham began preaching about the same time that a nation of neo-Pharisees hijacked the name *Israel*. Since then they have used their influence to create a climate of fear and political correctness, one in which they and only they are promoted as "Semites" and, "Israel." This, despite, as their own historians admit, they are not Israelites.

Your Responsibilities Now

As a professing Christian you are now without excuse. No longer can say you are not an Israelite, that you are not, therefore, among those *to whom pertaineth* the rights and responsibilities listed in Romans 9:4. Neither should you remain silent as your kindred succumb to a teaching which keeps them ignorant of the fact that *sin is the transgression of the law* (1 John 3:4); of the fact that to repent (Biblically) we must not make a practice of transgressing the law *(sin)*. You are obligated to warn your fellow Christian Israelites of a teaching which tells them they are "saved," that they are "born again," while ignoring the reason why Jesus will say, *I never knew you: depart from me, ye that work iniquity* (Matt. 7:22-23).

No, you are not required to keep *the law of the Lord* perfectly, Jesus did this for you. But, he does expect you to use it as your moral compass. He also expects our country's leaders to use the statutes and judgments of this law as a divine constitution, as a moral compass for the nation. A good way for them to start would be to implement the reforms made under Ezra and Nehemiah when the remnant of Judah returned from Babylon. These corrections involved three specific sins.

In the category of money, marriage, and commerce, they are rampant in the church and in the nation today. They are rampant because evangelicals, having caved in to political correctness, condone them. It is unlikely, however, that many among them will repent of their false teaching and speak against what is now institutionalized in the church and in the nation. And sadly, if they did, many in their congregations would probably leave and seek a preacher who does not speak against these sins. As the prophet Jeremiah stated, and applicable today:

> A wonderful and horrible thing is committed in the land; The prophets (teachers) prophesy (teach) falsely, and the priests bear rule by their means; *and my people love to have it so:* and what will ye do in the end thereof?
> Jeremiah 5:31 (parentheses, emphasis mine)

Be a Light to the World

As Jesus stated, we are, or are supposed to be, *the light of the world* (Matt. 5:14). As Israelites and as a nation in which a majority are yet Israelites, we are supposed to be a shining example of obedience to the Law of the Lord. We are supposed to *delight in the law of the Lord* (Psalm 1:2) and meditate in these precepts. To be reassured of the divine nature and of the perpetuity of this law, read the following excerpts from Psalm 119:

> Blessed are the undefiled in the way, *who walk in the law of the Lord.* Blessed are they that keep his testimonies, and that seek him with the whole heart. They also do no iniquity: they walk in his ways. Thou hast commanded us to keep thy precepts diligently. O that my ways were directed to keep thy statutes! Then shall I not be ashamed, when I have respect unto all thy commandments. I will praise thee with uprightness of heart, when I shall have learned thy righteous judgments. I will keep thy statutes: O forsake me not utterly.
>
> Psalm119:1-8 (emphasis mine)

> Thy word (law) have I hid in mine heart, that I might not sin against thee. Blessed art thou, O Lord: teach me thy statutes.... I will meditate in thy precepts, and have respect unto all thy ways. I will delight myself in thy statutes: *I will not forget thy law.*
>
> vv. 11-12; 15-16 (emphasis, parenthesis mine)

> Open mine eyes, that I may behold wondrous things out of thy law. I am a stranger in the earth: hide not thy commandments from me.   vv. 18-19

> O how love I thy law! It is my meditation all the day. Thou, through thy commandments hast made me wiser than mine enemies.   vv. 97-98

> Thy word (law) is a lamp unto my feet, and a light unto my path.... I have inclined mine heart to perform thy statutes always, even unto the end.
>
> vv. 105, 112 (parenthesis mine)

> Salvation is far from the wicked: for they seek not thy
> statutes.... Thy word is true from the beginning: and
> every one of thy righteous judgments endureth for
> ever.   vv. 155, 160

And on it goes for 176 verses. The Law of the Lord is so important that the entirety of the longest chapter in the Bible addresses this subject. As an Israelite, as one *to whom pertaineth* this law (Rom. 9:4), you should desire to learn of these precepts. In taking an honest look at it you will debunk a dominant interpretation, one which implies they have no practical application for today. It is upon discovering the relevance of this law that you will understand and accept the entire gospel, *the gospel of the kingdom* (Matt. 4:23) as taught by the Lord Jesus and the New Testament writers.

Understanding, then, the relevance of this law you will make a connection between the *curses,* between the consequences of disobedience prophesied in Deuteronomy 28 and America's decline. You will understand why Hosea wrote: *My people are destroyed for lack of knowledge*, and that this is because, as stated in the rest of the verse—*thou hast forgotten the law of thy God.* Discovering this truth you will desire to expose a lie, one which tells us that God is cursing America, not because our nation has abandoned his law as our moral compass, but—because we are not adequately supporting the Israelis. It will be difficult for you to remain silent as your fellow Christian Israelites apply Genesis 12:3 to a counterfeit Israel.

Expect Persecution

As an Israelite you cannot be a light to the world if you put these truths *under a bushel.* When you *let your light,* your obedience to God's law *so shine before men* that they *see your good works* you will be considered controversial. This is especially true when you, because the clergy do not, warn your fellow Christians regarding the sins addressed in Ezra and Nehemiah.

When you warn against these sins—three specific sins—you will be persecuted. You will be told you have been deceived, that these prohibitions regarding money, marriage, and commerce do not apply to us. You will be called before your pastor and church officers who, with dispensational-type arguments, will attempt to convince you that Ezra and Nehemiah—that *all scripture* (2 Tim. 3:16)—is somehow not profitable for reproof, for correction, for instruction in righteousness. Having, *by good words and fair speeches deceived the hearts of the simple* (Rom. 16:18), they will try the same on you. Invoking the mantra of dispensationalism they will say, "Because Israel rejected Jesus," the prohibitions described in Ezra and Nehemiah do not apply to the church, (Christians) that they were given to someone else.

When you explain that Israel did not reject Jesus, that the premise for their argument is wrong, they will respond as taught in seminary; they will accuse you of falling for some type of "Israelism." This, they will imply, is rooted in some other type of "ism," one which they will warn you against by invoking their interpretation of: *I will bless them that bless thee, and curse him that curseth thee* (Gen. 12:3). When this happens, when they resort to circular reasoning, it would be best to end the discussion, as any further argument on your part will be of no avail. The best way to do this is to ask if they have ever read a book on this subject; if they have honestly examined the other side of the story (very few have). You should then politely ask if they would read what convinced you and offer to lend them your copy of this book.

There is a chance that someone who pastors a small independent-type evangelical church will honestly examine whether or not Israel rejected Jesus two thousand years ago. This type of preacher is more flexible; is not dictated by denominational leaders. He will, unfortunately, limit the truth he preaches to a level acceptable by his congregation. This is because laypeople tend to have *itching ears*

(2 Tim. 4:3). Preferring *smooth things* (Isaiah 30:10), they do not always tolerate the whole truth and nothing but.

This is especially true regarding the three sins corrected by Ezra and Nehemiah. We are at a point in time when most Christians will not hear and do not respect these laws of the Lord—his restrictions on money, marriage, and commerce. This is especially true regarding mixed marriages. Many Christians, having heard the politically correct side only on this issue, have fallen for it and are literally ashamed of God's Word on the subject. Others are not, but fearful of being smeared with the "R" word, remain silent as this sin is condoned and even promoted by those who are supposed to oppose it.

The wicked, by smearing those who stand against sin as "haters" and "hate groups," have created a climate of fear in America. *In great power, and spreading...like a green bay tree* (Psalm 37:35) their influence in government, media, education, entertainment, and, yes, religion, is to the extent that most Christians are allowing political correctness to redefine right and wrong. Having abandoned the Law of the Lord as their moral compass, they are joining hands with the world as they justify sin and condemn righteousness. This is the anomia crowd, those who, *call evil good, and good evil; that put darkness for light, and light for darkness...; wise in their own eyes and prudent in their own sight they have cast away the law of the Lord of hosts, and despised the word of the Holy one of Israel* (Isaiah 5:20, 21, 24).

Put on the whole armour of God and get ready for persecution, for you will be persecuted *for righteousness' sake* when you stand up for the Law of the Lord.

They Will Question Your Salvation

Another method used against those who discover the gospel of the kingdom and the correct identity of Israel is to question their salvation. Certain teachers, when they cannot defend their dispensational-futurist mantras with Scripture logic and reason, will want to change the subject. Motivated by a desire to discredit the message, they will attempt to discredit the messenger. This is often done by attempting to change the subject, by questioning whether or not you are *saved*, and *born again.*

The questioning of your salvation status will often begin with a reminder that we are saved by grace, not by the works of the law, and that we are not under the law, but under grace. While this is true, their accusation that you are trying to obtain salvation by obeying the Law of the Lord is not. Remind your inquisitors that Christian-Israel believers, as much or more than they, recognize faith alone in the blood of the Lord Jesus Christ as sufficient for salvation. Remind them that we respect the Law of the Lord and use it as a moral compass, not to obtain salvation, but because we are repentant and are therefore led and indwelt by the Holy Spirit.

Yes, Romans 3:28 says, *a man is justified by faith without the deeds of the law,* but this does not contradict Romans 2:13 which says *doers of the law shall be justified.* Again, God's

> They avoid sin by using the Law of the Lord as their moral compass.

Word does not contradict itself; we cannot cling to either of these verses while ignoring the other. We must reconcile what Paul said in 3:28 with his earlier and related statement in 2:13. Paul was teaching that faith alone in Christ's work is sufficient for salvation, but that this faith does not *make void the law* (3:31). True faith is followed by obedience. By reconciling these seeming contradictions, we know *doers of the law shall be justified* because it is evidence of repentance, Biblical repentance. This means they are not abusing their pardon. Having obtained forgiveness they avoid sin by using the Law of the Lord as their moral compass.

Paul's statement, *We are not under the law,* does not mean what antinomian teachers imply. It is not a license to sin, to transgress the law with impunity. What Paul meant when writing *ye are not under the law* varies depending upon context. It can be a reminder that those of whom it was stated were no longer under the Old Covenant ceremonial portion of the law, or that because we are *under grace* (forgiveness) that we are not under the penalty of the law (death). In either case it does not nullify sin as *the transgression of the law,* or death, as *the wages of sin.*

Antinomian teachers create confusion by not differing between the blood ordinances, between the Old Covenant ceremonial portion of the law and the statutes or moral portion. Galatians 3:19, which follows, is an example where *law*—in context—emphasizes, not that which defines sin, but the Old Covenant rituals, the ceremonial law only:

> Wherefore then serveth the law (ceremonial)? It was added because of transgressions (of the moral law), till the seed should come to whom the promise was made; and it was ordained by angels in the hand of a mediator.   Galatians 3:19 (parentheses mine)

It will be necessary to remind antinomian teachers that it was sin (i.e., transgressions of the moral law) which made it necessary to add the rituals and blood ordinances (the ceremonial law), but only until *the seed should come to whom the promise was made.* Paul, in writing the Galatians, was not telling them that sin was no longer *the transgression of the law.* He was explaining the superiority of Israel's Messiah, of the works of Christ over the Old Covenant ceremonial portion of the law. Thus is the theme in Galatians; it is a contrast between the Old Covenant ceremonial portion of the law and the remaining moral law. These are not one and the same.

One cannot honestly say that the moral law, a summary of which is the Ten Commandments, was abrogated, or in other words, that Jesus came to *destroy the law* (Matt. 5:17). Messiah clearly warned against this teaching—one which results in lawlessness. It is given as the reason why, in that day, He will say, *I never knew you: depart from me, ye that work iniquity* [17] (Matt. 7:23). Jesus will say he never *knew* them; that he never acknowledged these Christians, because they practiced lawlessness (*iniquity*). They read the Sermon on the Mount, they read His sayings on the Law of the Lord, but because they *doeth them not, shall be likened unto a foolish man which built his house upon the sand...and it fell and great was the fall of it* (7:26).

Do not, then, allow dispensationalist/antinomian teachers to question your salvation—question theirs.

Born Again, by an Altar Call Ritual?

Also implied by most but not all dispensationalists is that *saved* defines someone who has responded to a Billy Graham-type altar call, or to someone who, (in their words) "asked Jesus into their heart," or, "received Christ as their personal Lord and Saviour," and/or variations of the same. These manmade one-time rituals are not without merit, however, and this is the problem; they have become an idol.

Whereas 1 John 2:3 says we know Jesus *if we keep his commandments,* millions of evangelicals now think they *know him* because they responded to an altar call or (in their words), "asked Jesus into my heart," or "received Christ into my life." These rituals have become substitutes, substitutes for the Jesus who commanded us to obey the Law of the Lord, who commanded us to use it (as he did) for our moral compass. Consider:

---

[17] #458 in *Strong's Concordance,* "iniquity" is translated from "anomia," i.e., lawlessness, transgression of the law, unrighteousness.

> If ye love me keep my commandments. And I will pray
> the Father, and he shall give you another Comforter....
> Even the Spirit of truth.   John 14:15; 16; 17

> And we are his witnesses of these things; and so is
> also the Holy Ghost, whom God hath given to them
> that obey him.   Acts 5:32

> Then Peter said unto them, Repent (of lawlessness)
> and be baptized every one of you in the name of Jesus
> Christ for the remission of sins, and ye shall receive
> the gift of the Holy Ghost.
>   Acts 2:38 (parenthesis mine)

Contrary, then, to antinomian teaching, when Christ says
those awful words, *I never knew you,* it will not be because
those in this category did not respond to a Billy Graham-type
altar call, or "ask Jesus into their heart." These are manmade
rituals; they are not evidence that one has been *born again.*

From Historicist to Futurist

In the course of examining scores of Scripture texts, we have
exposed a massive theological error, an idea, until now, we
blindly accepted. Because it was the only explanation given,
and because it was presented as a fact not open to debate,
we should have been suspicious. We should have searched
the Scriptures, whether it was so that those who accepted
Jesus two thousand years ago were not Israelites. But we did
not, and an error became the foundation for other errors.

We scrutinize Catholic, Mormon, Jehovah's Witness, and
other teachings, but too often, not that of our own church
or denomination. This is like leaving a door partially open;
it allows things to creep in. And they have; interpretations
have crept in that were unknown until recent generations.
History proves that the early church fathers and virtually
all Protestants until 1900 used the historicist approach
when interpreting Daniel's seventieth-week prophecy
and chapters 4-19 in the book of Revelation. But the

dispensationalist-futurist interpretation now prevails and we are in the second and third generation of evangelicals who have not heard the other side of the story, who grew up hearing futurism only. They have not heard the historicist, the classical Protestant interpretation of end-time events. They need to know that when Jesus descends from heaven the second time there is no second chance—that there is no third time seven years later.

The Difference Knowing Our Identity Makes

Because we have different responsibilities, it is important to know who we are. An adult knows that his or her responsibilities are greater than those of a child. Someone in a management position knows that his role and responsibility differs from those of the rank and file. For similar reasons we, the Anglo-Saxon, Celtic, Germanic, Scandinavian, and related Europeans, need to be aware of our Israelite origin. We, *of all the families of the earth,* are those whose responsibility it is to obey the Law of the Lord. The longer we deny this responsibility, the more of us there will be who hear those awful words. Consider again Christ's prophetic warning:

> Not every one that saith unto me, Lord, Lord, shall enter into the kingdom of heaven; but he that doeth the will of my Father which is in heaven. Many will say to me in that day, Lord, Lord, have we not prophesied in thy name? and in thy name have cast out devils? and in thy name done many wonderful works? And then will I profess unto them, *I never knew you: depart from me, ye that work iniquity* (anomia/lawlessness).
> Matthew 7:21-23 (parenthesis, emphasis mine)

The words *who work iniquity* would not be descriptive of Christians if they were not also describing *Israelites: to whom pertaineth...the law.* No longer can we pretend the Law of the Lord is not for us, that it pertains to the Israel of Judeo-Christian interpretations. These verses clearly identify professing Christians—a people those currently masquerading as Israel are not.

And, then, is 2 Chronicles 7:14. Knowing we are Israelites, the people to whom this was written is the key to under-standing this text:

> If my people, which are called by my name, shall humble themselves, and pray, and seek my face, and turn from their wicked ways; then will I hear from heaven, and will forgive their sin, and will heal their land.   2 Chronicles 7:14

Volumes could be written on this one text, a verse on how to repent, as an individual and—as a nation. Many of our national sins: legalized aborticide, sodomy, adultery, pornography, etc., are recognized and are opposed by evangelical Christians. But others, like those described in the books of Ezra and Nehemiah, are not; one in particular.

Thou Shalt Not Lend Upon Usury

Usury, as defined in Scripture, is the lending of money or things of value at interest. When a person *putteth...out his money to usury* (Psalm 15:5) for someone to use, and under the condition that the user pay a percentage over and above what was borrowed, *usury* is committed. Historically, this practice was forbidden among Christians until about the sixteenth century when it crept in and gained acceptance through negligent church leaders, John Calvin being its primary impetus.

Using money to increase—to multiply itself—was one of the reasons Jesus upset the tables of the moneychangers and drove them out of the temple (Mark 11:15). In Matthew 25:26-27 and Luke 19:22-23 usury is described as reaping what one has not sown. This agrees with other Scripture references, Ezekiel 18:8, 13, 17, and 22:12 in particular. In Proverbs 28:8 is a reference to *usury and unjust gain*. This type of gain is unjust because: One hundred dollars put out to *usury* at a rate of 10 percent for one year requires the user to repay $110. We know where the borrower gets the $100: from the lender. But where does one obtain the $10 needed as *usury*, as interest owed on the loan? The borrower, in the vast majority of cases, will have to work for it.

"Work" means they will produce a product or perform a service in exchange for the $10 the lender will receive as *usury*. Thus is the interest the *usury* portion of the loan

> Christ, in telling this parable, did not condone usury—he condemned it.

earned/worked for by the borrower—but not by the lender. This is why, in the parable of the talents, the using of money to buy and sell goods for profit (trading) is described as honorable—but the putting of money out to usury as not. When the servant's lord said: *Thou oughtest therefore to have put my money to the exchangers,*[18] *and then at my coming I should have received mine own with usury* (Matt. 25:27), it was in response to an excuse used by the unprofitable servant. The man had suggested that his lord was *a hard man, reaping where thou hast not sown.* It was then explained that if the servant really thought this were so he would not have buried, but increased the money by putting it out to usury. Christ, in telling this parable, did not condone usury—he condemned it. This was the real Jesus, He who said: *Think not that I am come to destroy the law* (Matt. 5:17).

We hear the term "interest earned," but this is an oxymoron for interest, because it is not acquired through the work process, is never earned. The result of a nation or economy where the exchange medium is continuously filtered through cycles of interest-bearing loans is that money becomes disproportionately owned by the lending class. It is then used by them to influence a nation's political process. A quick way to develop an understanding of

---

[18] "Exchangers" is Strong's #5133, *"trapezites: a money broker or banker."*

this is a Web search for—*Billions for the Bankers, Debts for the People*—a short, illustrated booklet which can be read online for free.

Also in agreement with prohibitions on usury is Christ's reminder to lend, hoping not for interest, but *nothing again* (Luke 6:35). But we ignore these warnings and justify this practice, largely, by assuming we are not Israelites, that Biblical references prohibiting usury apply to someone else. As a result this sin has institutionalized, has permeated almost every aspect of our economy and our lives.

One of its more obvious symptoms is that we are now taxed several hundred billion dollars annually just to pay interest on a national debt of $17 trillion and rising, and with no hope in sight. Sensing that something is wrong we blame it on the private "Federal" Reserve bankers and their debt-money system. But the root of the problem is sin—the sin of institutionalized usury. Our ignorance and our defiance of this and other areas of God's law is why *My people are destroyed for lack of knowledge.* Until we turn from our wicked ways, until we seek His face and make illegal this sin, it will continue to rob and enslave us.

Knowing, then, we are Israelites makes a difference—the difference between knowing our responsibilities and not. We can no longer pretend, because we are Christians; we are not those *to whom pertaineth...the law* and that John's reminder *(for sin is the transgression of the law)* is for someone else. This will be no excuse when, *The Son of man shall send forth his angels, and they shall gather out of his kingdom all things that offend, and them which do iniquity* (lawlessness).

Another Nontraditional Marriage

Iniquity/lawlessness/sin increases when legalized by government. We saw this happen when the US Supreme Court declared as unconstitutional restrictions on aborticide

(Roe v. Wade, 1973) and sodomy (Lawrence v. Texas, 2003). Given legal protection, these sins exploded. They are, however, not the first sins to be given legal protection. There are many others, some of which have become so common they are considered respectable and no longer recognized as sin.

Examples of these are the three mentioned in Ezra and Nehemiah, those adopted while in the Babylonian captivity. Younger people, especially, are accepting of these. Having not lived at a time when they were also prohibited by man's law, and because their church does not preach against them, they see no evil in such practices.

It will also be noticed that certain sins, once given legal protection, are used by the wicked as evidence, as case examples when arguing why other sins should be legalized. This is illustrated by the way homosexuals and lesbians use Virginia v. Loving, the Supreme Court case which nullified state laws prohibiting mixed marriage. It, they argue, is reason why same-sex couples also should be allowed to marry. With Hollywood, the mainstream news media, public education, and the judicial system on their side, they are getting closer to this every day. As with Virginia v. Loving in 1967, this will probably occur as a US Supreme Court decision, one which will strike down all restrictions against same-sex marriage. When this occurs, when same-sex couples also are given "civil rights" protection and churches are pressured to comply with political correctness, most will probably succumb and accept this sin. Having accepted others, it is likely they will accept this one also, and another sin will become respectable.

May God spare us from the eventual destruction of today's Sodom and Gomorrah. May He forgive the rest of us if and when same-sex couples are "married," are legally but sinfully joined together in church wedding ceremonies.

Lawlessness, a Mark of the Beast

It is upon understanding that we are Israelites, that we are those *to whom pertaineth,* that we also understand why *my people are destroyed for lack of knowledge.* Until Jesus returns, this lack of knowledge and resultant destruction will continue as *Mystery, Babylon the Great,* as the current economic, political, and religious system rules over us. Thanks to the dispensational-futurist prophetic interpretation, Mystery Babylon is a "mystery," is unrecognized by most evangelicals. Not understanding that *the mystery of iniquity* (lawlessness) *doth already work* (2 Thess. 2:7), and, because their focus is on a Babylon in some future-only, seven-year period, they do not recognize that *things that offend* (Matt. 13:41) describe government sanctioned lawlessness—in a system operating now. Neither do they seem to recognize *the tares,* the wicked among us who are the architects and ringleaders of this lawless beast system.

> Mystery Babylon is a "mystery," is unrecognized by most evangelicals.

The book of Revelation, more than other New Testament writings, contains terms and phrases relating to the history of Israel. It is a book of prophecy, a "revelation" of future events concerning God's covenant people. Once we know they did not reject Jesus, that the church was and is an institution within Israel, we will interpret this book using the historicist view, the classical Protestant interpretation. We will not use the futurist view. We will not have to futurize and compress sixteen chapters (4-19) of Revelation into some seven-year-only period, in an attempt to make these fit a counterfeit Israel, a nation of neo-Pharisees in old Palestine.

In chapter 12 Israel is symbolized by a sun-clad woman and Mystery Babylon by a dragon. It concludes:

> And the dragon was wroth with the woman, and went to make war with the remnant of her seed, which *keep the commandments of God,* and have the testimony of Jesus Christ.
>
> Revelation 12:17 (emphasis mine)

This theme continues through chapter 13, where the dragon gives power unto a beast (a beast system) whose number *is the number of a man; and his number is six hundred three-score and six.* It is stated of those who worship this system that they will have its mark in their forehead, in their hand, and will drink of the wine of the wrath of God.

Opposite those who receive this mark of the beast are they who have the name of God *written in their foreheads* (Rev. 14:1). It, as the mark of the beast in one's forehead, is not necessarily literal. It is probably best understood in relation to Deuteronomy 6:5-9 and other texts, those with references to the Law of the Lord *in thine heart; upon thine hand; between thine eyes,* etc. In their heart (mind) and between their eyes were other words for *in their foreheads* or—in their minds.

It stands, then, to reason that the mark of the beast, the economic, political, and religious beast system, is probably not a tattoo on or a RFID (Radio-Frequency IDentification) device in someone. It would be something in one's forehead (beliefs), or in their right hand (actions) which "mark" them as opposites of *the remnant of her seed which keep the commandments of God.* Not keeping the commandments, i.e., not using them as one's moral standard, is also defined as iniquity/lawlessness and therefore would be a mark of the beast, a lawless beast system. This is the exact opposite of *the kingdom of God,* the Christian theocracy based upon the Law of the Lord.

Because we cannot perfectly obey the commandments of God and are under grace does not mean, as antinomian teachers imply, that we are at liberty to abandon them. *Keep,* in this context means, not perfectly, but—as a moral standard. And, there are more than ten. The Decalogue, or the Ten Commandments, are not the entirety of God's law; they are a summary only, a summary of its statutes in a given area. Usury, for example, and prohibitions thereof are a statue of the eighth commandment *(Thou shalt not steal)*. Aborticide, or induced abortion, is prohibited by the sixth *(Thou shalt not kill)*. Prohibitions against premarital sex are statutes of the seventh *(Thou shalt not commit adultery)*.

Gambling, another sin legalized in recent times, would be prohibited under the tenth commandment *(Thou shalt not covet)*. Also sin, but legalized in recent times, is pornography. Yes, there are thought sins which pornography is and they are prohibited under the seventh commandment *(Thou shalt not commit adultery)*. These are but a few examples of *things that offend,* of government-sanctioned lawlessness by an anti-Christ system. To participate in them is to *do iniquity* (lawlessness) and is likely a mark, if not *the* mark of a beast—the eighth beast in a system called *Mystery, Babylon the Great.*

> *Why call me, Lord, Lord, and do not the things which I say?*

Those who do not keep the commandments of God, and who receive the mark of the beast, are basically one and the same with those of whom Jesus said, *why call me, Lord, Lord, and do not the things which I say?* (Luke 6:46). These are the disobedient, the antinomian Christians of whom He will say, *I never knew you: depart from me, ye that work iniquity (lawlessness).*

It cannot be emphasized too strongly that the above statements by Jesus are not prophetic of Muslims, Hindus, or Buddhists, i.e., of other *families of the earth.* They are descriptive of those among Christendom who are tempted, and who have fallen for the permissiveness of antinomian teaching. They are following apostate church and denominational leaders, those who ignore and deny that *sin is the transgression of the law*—the Law of the Lord. Having been lead into temptation they have fallen for the antinomian interpretation, one implying, that because we cannot perfectly obey the commandments of God, we do not have to *keep* them as our moral standard.

What Happened to Sunday?

In recent years, certain dispensationalists have boldly added to a roster of antinomian interpretations. The Ten Commandments, it seems, are now reduced to nine. They are claiming that the fourth *(Remember the Sabbath day, to keep it holy)* died on the cross with Jesus and was not reinstituted. Whether or not this commandment applies to the historical Sunday, or to another day is, in their opinion, no longer a moot issue since they are now saying it was abrogated.

This teaching crept in among evangelicals after World War II as stores and restaurants began opening on Sunday. When the practice began, store and restaurant employees could still go to church because the businesses did not open until noon, but now it is ten o'clock and earlier. Some are open the entire twenty-four hours on Sunday. In his book, *D. L. Moody on The Ten Commandments,*[19] the late D. L. Moody describes how, while in France, he could not tell one day from another, "On Sunday, stores were open and buildings were erected, the same as on other days" (p. 62). Few of today's evangelical leaders follow Moody's teaching regarding Sunday and the fourth commandment. The last edition of his book was published in 1977.

Although he would not have been the first to do so, TV evangelist Jimmy Swaggart was heard reducing the Ten Commandments to nine by this writer in the early 1980s. Just recently Dr. John C. Whitcomb, in a question-and-answer

---

[19] D. L. Moody, *D. L. Moody on the Ten Commandments* (Chicago: Moody Press, 1896).

program on Worldview Weekend Radio, was heard reducing the Ten to nine. Whitcomb, born about 1924, would well remember (and why) when most stores and restaurants were closed on Sunday. That their position on the fourth commandment is contrary to over 1,900 years of church teaching on this subject seems not to bother dispensational-ists. To be commended, however, for not selling *victuals and wares* on Sunday are the Christian owned and controlled Chick-fil-A restaurants and Hobby Lobby stores. They do not open their doors on the Christian Sabbath.

Of the hundreds of Sunday-closing laws ("blue laws") once in the nation's statute books, few remain, or are enforced. Even alcoholic beverages, once widely restricted on Sunday, are now becoming available the entire week. In my home state of Wisconsin auto dealers are among the few businesses to not open their doors this one day in seven. The historical Christian Sabbath, in less than two generations, has become a major day for the selling of victuals and wares—as *the prophets prophesy falsely...and my people love to have it so.*

Multiculturalism, a Tool of the Beast

Among *things which offend* and which contribute to the decline and fall of Christianity in America is multicultur-alism. One and the same with "diversity" and "pluralism," multiculturalism is the agenda of those who desire many religions/cultures in a locality without any one culture or religion dominating the region. A motto promoting this agenda is "Celebrate Diversity." Also used (on a rainbow background) by promoters of the homosexual and lesbian agenda, this motto is seen on cars, on billboards, and in public schools. Promoters of "diversity" are often heard crying for "tolerance," a hypocritical stance on their part since they also are intolerant when anyone resists the imposing of their values.

This is reflected by their labeling of those who oppose them, in any organized way as "hate groups." Major news outlets, the Anti-Defamation League, and the Southern Poverty Law Center, being cheerleaders for their cause, will then repeat, ad nauseam, these "hate group" charges. Hate, according to these shadowy

> Multiculturalism...
> is a euphemism for a
> strategy known as—
> divide and conquer.

anti-Christian organizations, is a factual, well-reasoned Biblical argument. It does not take much in the way of discernment to recognize that multiculturalism is a code word, a euphemism for a strategy known as—divide and conquer.

The Bible has much to say about the mixing of *the heathen,* of other cultures and their gods with *my people,* with God's Israel covenant people, and it is all negative. Latter-day Christian Israelites are mostly unaware this, or if they are, assume these restrictions do not apply to them. They may recognize what multiculturalism is doing to their country, but because they are taught the fallacy that they also are of *heathen* non-Israelitish ancestry they assume there is no Biblical argument against it. Thus is another example of how *my people,* because we do not know we are Israelites, *are destroyed for lack of knowledge.*

A good way to acquire Biblical knowledge regarding *the heathen* and their gods is a Berean type search for *heathen* in Scripture. This is easily done by using *Strong's Exhaustive Concordance,* the book, or in whole verse form at *blueletterbible.com.* By following this word verse by verse in its original context you will understand what the Bible says regarding multiculturalism.

What then, could be a more insidious way to dethrone Christianity as a primary influence than the using of anti-Christian activists in the judiciary to force-feed us multiculturalism? While Western-Christian culture yet dominates in America it is in rapid decline as the anti-Christ beast system welcomes *the heathen* and their gods. Do not, therefore, "celebrate diversity," do not celebrate the decline of traditional Christian values in America.

Who Controls the Present Beast System?

We understand, then, why those who promote the futurist interpretation of Revelation also repeat *anti-Christ* as "the Anti-Christ," as future and one man. By repeating and emphasizing this word as a proper noun, and as one and the same with a future-only beast, they are attempting to divert attention from anyone today. What they are saying is, "Don't worry about anyone or anything now; the beast and the anti-Christ do not appear until after the rapture." Who does the futurist interpretation allow to fly in—under the radar? It is none other than the architects and enforcers of *things that offend,* of government-sanctioned sin/lawlessness. As *anti-Christs,* and as administrators of a mystery called *Mystery, Babylon the Great,* it is they who are the chief beneficiaries of the dispensationalist-futurist interpretation. *In great power, and spreading...like a green bay tree,* the wicked must laugh as evangelicals, focused on a future-only *beast* and *anti-Christ,* are oblivious to their presence.

Jesus said, *occupy till I come* (Luke 19:13), but in our naivety we allow the opposite. Of those who occupy the seats of government in our nation's capital, few if any are Bible-believing Christians. Every four years we choose between two presidential candidates, each of whom is always some type of professing Christian. But we seem not to notice when our newly elected "Christian" betrays us by surrounding himself with non-Christian and openly anti-Christ people. Why? Have we been lulled into complacency by the futurist interpretation? Are we so focused on a future-only *beast* and *anti-Christ* that we do not recognize *the wicked* in control? We may *occupy,* but it is mostly church pews on Sunday. Virtually no Bible-believing Christians are appointed to high-level positions in Washington DC—*tares* only need apply.

By their fruits ye shall know them (Matt. 7:20). While originally stated regarding false teachers, this principle is applicable in other areas. One of the evil fruits brought forth by the mainstream news media is a silent approval when Christians are excluded from presidential appointments. Quick to bark, when others are discriminated against, the media "watchdogs" are suspiciously silent when Christians are excluded.

Another of their evil fruits is the so-called "separation of church and state." Despite the fact that none of these words appear in the establishment clause (Amendment I, US Constitution), they are repeated as a substitute for those which do. Millions of Americans do not realize that this oft-repeated phrase by a wishful-thinking news media is an interpretation only. The words "separation of church and state" appear, not in the establishment clause, but in the Marxist constitution of the old Soviet Union.

In support of futurism and computer chip implants as the mark of the beast is that RFIDs were not possible until recent years. And, it is true that the wicked, that those who control the present-day New World Order, would like for us a microchip implant. But, it is not true that such would be a mystery to those implanted. What does seem to be a mystery, something not understood by most evangelicals, is the number of innocent people killed by wicked governments and religious rulers since the book of Revelation was written.

First, and lasting through the third century, were the Roman persecutions of Christians. When the Roman Empire fell, Christians were no longer fed to lions but were soon persecuted in other ways by the Roman papal system. Known in history as the Inquisition, these persecutions began about in the sixth century and lasted into the seventeenth. During this time Roman papal authorities abused, tortured, and murdered even more Christians than the previous Roman system.

Pastor Charles Jennings of Kingdom Treasure Ministries in Owasso, Oklahoma, has written a commentary on the Book of Revelation.[20] Using the classical historicist interpretation of prophecy, Pastor Jennings explains how five world empires, Egypt, Assyria, Babylon, and Medo-Persia, were *fallen* (Rev. 17:10) when John received the Revelation prophecy. Described as *one is* (v. 10) was the sixth world empire, Imperial Rome (because it was presently in existence). The seventh world empire, that which was *yet to come* (v.10) when the Revelation was received, was the empire of papal Rome. As Pastor Jennings further explains:

> The angel identifies these seven world empires as **heads** but in verse 11 the angel mentions a beast which contains all of the seven heads plus the body of the beast. This beast is considered to be the eighth because he is the personification and the incarnation of the seven previous world empires. This beast that has been identified as being the very essence of the seven previous heads is none other than the present day New World Order.
>
> *The Book of Revelation: From an Israelite and Historicist Interpretation*, p. 200.

Tens of millions of Christians were persecuted, tortured, and murdered by Imperial Rome and in the inquisitions of its successor, papal Rome. As the Scriptures prophesy, these would have been times of *great tribulation.* This should not be confused with what those of the futurist interpretation call "the tribulation." In one only (Matt. 24:29) out of nineteen applications in the New Testament, is the word *tribulation* preceded by *the.* The other eighteen

---

[20] Charles A. Jennings, *The Book of Revelation, From An Israelite and Historicist Interpretation*, www.truthinhistory.org.

do not support an idea expressed as "the tribulation." As previously explained, there is no second chance in some future-only seven-year period. When Jesus descends from heaven (the second and last time) he is here to stay—in the kingdom of God on earth.

CHAPTER 16

THE NEW WORLD ORDER, THE LAST BEAST

Succeeding papal Rome in the 1700s is the eighth and last beast. It, too, is described as reigning *over the kings of the earth* (Rev. 17:18) and seems to be an incarnation of the previous empire but with additional political and economic characteristics. Headed by numerous old-world banking families and known (by those aware of it) as the New World Order, it operates as a type of invisible government. It does this, primarily, by establishing itself within a nation as its central bank. This position is then used to control the type and the issue of the nation's exchange medium and therefore its economy. Beginning with the Rothschild banking dynasty in the 1600s, this international cartel now operates as the central bank in most modern industrialized nations. As the Bank of England in the 1700s, they controlled the type and the issue of money in England and its colonies.

In 1776 thirteen of England's colonies broke free from it and the usury-bearing exchange medium they had been forced to use. From then onward the moneychangers would attempt to regain their former control by establishing a central bank in the US. This was known (and resisted) by Andrew Jackson, Abraham Lincoln, James Garfield, and William McKinley. Jackson survived assassination attempts; the others did not.

With passage of the Federal Reserve Act of 1913 the international bankers succeeded in gaining control of US monetary policy. In the same year, and also designed by the moneychangers, came a tax on wages (the "income tax"). This would supply the additional revenue government would need in order to pay usury charges on the credit and currency it would borrow through the Federal Reserve System. Shortly thereafter, and also for their benefit, would come the IRS (Internal Revenue Service). With it as their collection agency, the Fed moneychangers, without sowing anything, could now reap from the earnings of all who work.

As previously explained, usury paid on debt is earned, not by the lender—but by the borrower only. This is especially true regarding the usury collected on an exchange medium issued as debt instruments (fiat money, i.e., credit and nonredeemable currency). These do function as money, but are not bona fide because they are issued—without first being earned in the process called *work*.

The Fed's debt instruments, its currency and credit, do not represent the value of anyone's product or service. They are designed as a device to acquire a percentage of the wages earned by those who do produce a product or perform a service. Much of the tax on our labor (the "income tax") is received by moneylenders as usury on the national debt. Thus do the Fed moneychangers reap what they do not sow. They produce no food or fiber, manufacture no goods, and perform no necessary service, yet, by receiving usury, acquire a portion of the same from those who do. Here's how it works.

The Fed's Compared to Lincoln's Fiat Money

When the federal government needs to spend more than taken from us in taxes, it must borrow the money. If, for example there is a deficit of $100 billion, Congress must raise the debt limit and authorize the Treasury to issue that amount in debt instruments called bonds and notes. When purchased by the Fed, our government receives what is, essentially, credit—mostly in electronic form. This newly created "checkbook money" is then spent into circulation as the government pays its obligations.

Our government now owes the Fed $100 billion for which it must impose a tax on our labor to pay the interest. Thanks to legalized usury and the Federal Reserve debt-money system, hundreds of these transactions have resulted in our nation owing trillions of dollars on which "we the people" must pay annual interest—with no hope of ever paying the principle. That this growing debt cannot and will not be paid does not worry those who operate this Ponzi scheme. But then, why would it? The money they lend is created for next to nothing. Their primary concern is collecting the interest, not the principal.

It is not necessary for ours, or any government, to borrow its exchange medium from a private central bank. Congress, which created the Fed, can at any time, repeal the Federal Reserve Act and/or exercise its constitutional authority to coin money and regulate the value thereof (Article 1, section 8, clause 5) by ordering the Treasury to issue currency and credit directly to the government, debt/interest free. Once spent into circulation it would serve indefinitely as an exchange medium by recycling back to the government as taxes. This was done (with success) by Abraham Lincoln in 1863 with the issue of $450 million in fiat money called "greenbacks." As Lincoln stated:

Government, possessing the power to create and issue currency and credit...need not and should not borrow capital at interest as the means of financing governmental work and public enterprise.[21]

Abraham Lincoln

There is good reason to believe that the eighth and last beast in the book of Revelation is the current invisible government, or New World Order. Led by banking dynasties with names like Rothschild, Morgan, Rockefeller, etc., this cartel has used its wealth to buy control in major corporations. According to Henry Makow, Ph.D., and author of *Illuminati 2: Deceit & Seduction*: "It takes only 3 per cent to 4 per cent of shares to control most widely held corporations." As Makow explains; "These corporations, in turn, buy executives, politicians, pundits and professors that run the world for the bankers."

The CFR, a Front for the New World Order

An example of those who run the world for international bankers is the Council on Foreign Relations think tank. Founded in 1921, the semi-secret CFR has a membership of several thousand financial executives, academics, media executives, military officers, federal judiciary members, and other elites. Its purpose has been described as follows:

> The Council on Foreign Relations is the American branch of a society which organized in England... (and) ...believes national boundaries should be obliterated and one world rule established.[22]

US Senator Barry Goldwater

The society organized in England of which the CFR is a branch is the Royal Institute of International Affairs, a

---

[21] Excerpted: "An Abstract of Lincoln's Monetary Policy," certified as correct by the Legislative Reference Service of the Library of Congress.

[22] Barry M. Goldwater, *With No Apologies* (New York: Berkley Books), 126.

foreign policy-making front for the London-based Rothschild banking dynasty. On October 30, 1993, *The Washington Post* described the CFR as "the nearest thing we have to a ruling establishment...the people who, for more than half a century, have managed our international affairs and our military-industrial complex." This admission is rare for a mainstream news outlet, an organization whose editor and numerous writers are CFR members.

It does not require a great degree of discernment to recognize that those on the CFR membership roster are disproportionately atheistic or otherwise anti-Christ. In recent years prominent religious leaders such as Rick Warren (author, *The Purpose Driven Life*) and Richard Land (leader, Southern Baptist Convention) have been recruited into its ranks. But this is not to the CFR's credit. It only proves that those of the dispensationalist-futurist interpretation are of use to anti-Christ New World Order operatives.

It was neoconservative-type CFR members in the George W. Bush administration who planned and implemented the bombing and invasion of Iraq and the ongoing action in Afghanistan. The news anchors and political pundits whose edits and comments created support for these wars were also CFR members. Something smells when a mainstream news anchor interviews the secretary of state, defense, the treasury, or other departments and the audience is not told they are listening to one CFR member questioning another. This is clearly a conflict of interest and is not honest. An action, plan, or activity designed to undermine a nation's sovereignty, i.e., its constitution, is subversion, and is one of the definitions of conspiracy.

By 2008 the electorate was fed up with war and war-induced deficit spending by a Republican administration. Vulnerable to a candidate promising "Change," we elected someone little was known about. Among the things we did not know was that Barack Obama's "Change" would be a presidential cabinet again selected from the membership roster of the Council on Foreign Relations. Neither has the president's promise of "Change" resulted in a reduction in deficit spending. His deficits exceed those of his predecessor and are therefore even more profitable for the Fed bankers who finance them.

"Follow the money," as the old adage goes, and you will find those responsible for the problem. This was done (in retirement) by the decorated Marine Corps Major General Smedley Butler. His conclusion: *War is a Racket,*[23] a book describing regret for a career in which he unknowingly participated in military interventions for Wall Street interests. Similar conclusions were drawn by Henry Ford who stated: "Wars...are the work of a small group of men who profit by them."[24] Ford, who had not forgotten his humble farm boy beginnings, was a populist and advocate for the working class. He understood that war is a rich man's game and a poor man's fight.

There are other organizations, secret and semisecret, which operate as front groups for the international bankers and their Federal Reserve, but the CFR, because its members control mainstream news outlets, is their most important tool. It is a mistake, therefore, to assume, because we are not living under a Stalin or Hitler-type dictatorship, that someone is not using the mass media to influence public opinion.

One of the more obvious examples of this is the respect given by media elites to homosexual and lesbian causes. Multicultural advocates also, receive ample and positive coverage, but woe to anyone who takes a Biblical stand on these subjects. Their position will be dismissed as founded on some irrational fear ("homophobic," etc.), or on prejudice and hate. News outlets do this by interviewing organizations

---

[23] *War is a Racket,* by General Smedley Butler. The booklet and quotations thereof can be read online for free.

[24] *New Orleans Times-Picayune,* Meigs Frost interview, August 22, 1934.

such as the Anti-Defamation League and the Southern Poverty Law Center. During these interviews it is standard procedure for network news anchors to show a muted video clip of the accused—while the ADL or SPLC representative tells the audience what to think.

Behind Communism and Socialism

The origins of opposition to Western culture and the Christian religion from which it arose can be recognized in the following quote:

> How to Destroy the West: Corrupt the young. Get them away from religion. Encourage their interest in sex. Make them superficial by focusing their interests in sports, sensual entertainments and trivialities. Always preach true democracies but seize power as fast and ruthless as possible. Encourage government extravagance, destroy its credit. Produce fear with rising prices, inflation and general discontent. Encourage disorders and foster a lenient attitude toward disorders. By specious argument cause the breakdown of the old moral virtues: Honesty, sobriety and self-restraint. Cause the registration of firearms to leave the population defenseless.
>
> Vladimir Lenin, 1921

The first socialist/atheist totalitarian regime began as the Bolshevik Revolution in 1917. This was not, as we are commonly told, a grassroots uprising of oppressed Russian peasants. Do a computer search for "who financed communism" or, "who financed Lenin and Trotsky" and one will find pages of Web sites containing suppressed truth on this subject. While it is true that Lenin, Trotsky, and the trained revolutionaries who overthrew Czar Nicholas II once lived in Russia, their base was New York. It was from there, and with financing by Wall Street bankers, that they returned to murder the Czar, his family, his servants, and millions of others while creating their socialist, religion-free "workers paradise."

This financing of Marxist revolutionaries by wealthy bankers is well-documented by authors Antony Sutton,[25] G. Edward Griffin,[26] and others. According to Griffin, Jacob Schiff, head of the New York investment firm Kuhn, Loeb & Co., was a principle backer having provided Lenin and Trotsky with $20 million. Schiff, not surprisingly, was an advocate of the Federal Reserve Act and contributed large sums to the campaign of Woodrow Wilson, who signed it into law.

Bankers in Germany and England also were backing Lenin and Trotsky. These, as the newly organized Federal Reserve bankers, were in the Rothschild sphere of influence. Thanks to a source of uncensored information called the Internet, much scholarly information is now readily available on this subject.

It will not be explained in detail here but it is well documented that Rothschild banking interests were one and the same with England's attempt to regain America in 1812. General Andrew Jackson, one of our nation's greatest heroes, prevented this by winning the Battle of New Orleans. As President Jackson he again drove the Rothschild moneychangers out of America by vetoing the National Banking Act of 1836. Jackson, who survived two assassination attempts, was the first president to balance the Federal Budget. When Old Hickory left office he had only $90 in his pocket, but the nation had a $60 million surplus.

By 1857 international banking interests were again plotting against America. The moneychangers were afraid that if the thirty-four states remained united as one nation they would become an economic, financially independent giant which would upset their plans for financial domination of the

---

[25] Antony C. Sutton, *Wall Street and the Bolshevik Revolution*, 1974.

[26] G. Edward Griffin, *The Creature from Jekyll Island: A Second Look at the Federal Reserve*, chapter 13, pages 263-267.

world. Led by Rothschild interests they were implementing a plan to divide and conquer by exploiting the slavery issue. One Judah P. Benjamin, a wealthy lawyer and politician, was their primary front man.

Benjamin no longer owned his plantation and 140 slaves but remained loyal to the cause as he used it and his political clout to promote secession. Known by many historians as "the brains of the revolt," Benjamin was instrumental in convincing the South to secede from the Union. With this accomplished he served as Secretary of State and Secretary of War of the Confederacy. There is considerable evidence connecting Benjamin to the Confederate Secret Service and the assassination of Lincoln, but he was successful in fleeing to England before he could be captured and questioned.

Few Americans are aware of the role Czar Alexander II of Russia played in assisting Abraham Lincoln as the money power in Europe plotted against him. Also an emancipator, the czar, in 1861, had freed millions of Russians from the shackles of serfdom. Through his ambassadors in London and Paris, the Christian czar had learned of English and French plans to intervene on behalf of the Confederacy. To deter this he sent Russian naval forces to New York and San Francisco with instructions to take orders from Lincoln. It worked. England and France did not intervene and Lincoln, in defeating the South, preserved the Union.

Writing during the war, he described the European bankers and their plots as a greater foe than the Confederacy. Lincoln was murdered in 1865; his friend Czar Alexander in 1881 (after two attempts). The author is indebted to the late Eustace Mullins and his well-researched but suppressed book *The World Order* for much of this information.

An awareness of international banking and its role in history is crucial to recognizing the eighth and last beast of *Mystery, Babylon the Great.* This political, economic, and religious system began its rise as papal Rome, the seventh beast, began its fall in the 1600s. A characteristic of the current Babylonian beast system is its mysterious ability to operate unseen by millions of evangelical Christians. Contributing to this invisibility is the futurist interpretation, that which tells them to focus on the tribulations described in chapters 4-19 in Revelation as entirely yet to be. This is despite the fact that tens of millions of Christians have died as a result of religious and other persecution since the Revelation prophecies were written. Unlike futurism, the historicist, the classical Protestant interpretation of the Revelation prophecies, does not ignore history. For this reason it is not promoted by secretive New World Order elites who are one and the same with the eighth and last beast. They would rather operate incognito—behind the veil of futurism.

Had it not been for Czar Alexander II of Russia, the European bankers may have gotten their wish for a permanently divided thirty-four states. For this and other reasons they harbored a special hatred for Romanov, czarist Russia. By thus financing the Bolshevik Revolution they would get their revenge and other desires.

Czar Nicholas II, his wife, his children, their doctor, and their servants were murdered by Bolshevik anti-Christs on July 17, 1918. They were killed, execution style, on the direct orders of New York banker Jacob Schiff.[27] A computer search for "Jacob Schiff ordered czar and family murdered" will reveal pages of Web sites containing suppressed truth regarding this and other Bolshevik mass murders. The czar and his family were among the first of eight million Russian Orthodox Christians killed by atheistic Communism from 1918-1943.

---

[27] For documentation read, *Under the Sign of the Scorpion*, by Jüri Lina, pp. 276-277. This book is heavily suppressed but can be read for free on line.

Under Lenin and Stalin the number of churches went from 50,000 to less than 500 as the buildings were demolished. Tens of thousands of church leaders, declared enemies of the state, were sentenced to the Gulags and their deaths. To comply with Stalin's order that "the notion of God will be expunged," the teaching of religion in private homes was forbidden. The government, which took control all education, encouraged children to report parents who talked about religion at home. One can see the beginnings of a similar anti-Christian government policy in America as non-Christians grow in influence.

The following is a summary of an article written December 13, 1998, by Eric Margolis of the *Toronto Sun* editorial department. To read this article in its entirety, do a Web search for *Remembering Ukraine's Unknown Holocaust.*

In 1932 Russian Ukrainian peasants were yet resisting the collectivizing of agriculture. To remedy this Joseph Stalin sent in 25,000 Communist Party fanatics with orders to kill any and all connected with the resistance. Stalin's henchman, Lazar Kaganovich, was in charge of the genocide. When a quota of 10,000 executions per week was deemed insufficient, Kaganovich ordered mass starvation. Grain, seed stocks, livestock, and fuel where then confiscated as the same was prevented from coming in on roads and rail lines.

During the winter of 1932-33, which was particularly severe, Ukrainians were freezing and starving. When pets had been eaten, the diet was bark and grass; some even resorted to cannibalizing the deceased. As the Soviet Empire fell apart in 1991 KGB archives became open to Russian historians. The records revealed that at least seven million Ukrainians were shot, starved, and frozen to death by Stalin and his Bolshevik atheists during the early 1930s. During this time the US, British, and Canadian governments learned of the atrocity but did little or nothing to intervene. Also described as ignoring, and/or denying the genocide were major newspapers such as *The New York Times*. The author of said article describes their coverage of the event as—"a left-wing conspiracy of silence that continues to this day."

According to the best available statistics, the number of people executed, starved, and worked to death under Lenin and Stalin is a holocaust which exceeds that of Adolph Hitler by fourfold. Despite this far greater number of Christian and Russian victims, a secular establishment has succeeded in conditioning us to accept Hitler's killings only—as "the Holocaust."

The Twentieth, History's Bloodiest Century

Death by Government is the fourth in a series of books written by R. J. Rummel, professor of political science at the University of Hawaii. Building upon years of research, Rummel has compiled, what appears to be, the most complete statistics on twentieth-century genocide and mass murder. The following, taken from his Web site, can be verified by doing a search for *Death by Government: Genocide and Mass Murder.* In it he describes the murder of people by government, including genocide, politicide, and mass murder, as "democide." Rummel, according to Wikipedia, revived and redefined the term out of necessity for a word describing any and all murder by government.

According to Rummel's statistics, the victims of democide by the USSR from 1917-87 total over sixty million. The total for Nazi Germany in the years 1933-45 is twenty million. Not to be outdone by the Nazis is the People's Republic of China. "Chairman Mao" and his successors, from 1949-87, starved, shot, and otherwise killed over thirty-five million in a socialist totalitarian regime which is still operating today.

One of the more recent examples of murder by government occurred in 1975-79. This was the systematic killing of two million Cambodians by the atheist socialist dictator Pol Pot and his Khmer Rouge. During that time this writer remembers how NBC news anchor Tom Brokaw would open his nightly newscast with a blitzkrieg against, not the government of Cambodia, but South Africa. Apartheid, it seems, was a greater problem to the media elites than mass murder in Cambodia.

The Bolshevik Revolution was not the first democide of the twentieth century. This distinction was imposed upon two million Armenians by the Ottoman Turks. A separate community for over two thousand years, Armenia was one of the first nations to adopt Christianity as a state religion. By the tenth century Christianity in Armenia flourished to the extent that its capital, Ani, was called "the city of a thousand and one churches." But not long after, Armenians became outnumbered by a growing Muslim majority around them.

By the sixteenth century Armenians were more or less an ethnic and religious minority subject to the Turkish government. The persecutions began late in the nineteenth century. Triggered by political and economic pressures resulting from the decline in the Ottoman Empire, they continued, escalating further during World War I. During this conflict the Turks were siding with Germany against Russia. Part of the historic Armenian territory was in Russia and the Muslim Turks were accusing Armenians of affinities with Christian Russia.

> As a prelude to this ethnic/religious cleansing, Armenians were required to surrender all firearms.

Prior to, and as a prelude to this ethnic/religious cleansing, Armenians were required to surrender all firearms. The genocide then began. From April 1915 through 1918 the Christian Armenians went through a tribulation of massacres, death marches, and unspeakable atrocities. When they were gone the cleansing continued as priceless, irreplaceable old libraries and archives were destroyed. Entire cities, including the ancient capital of Ani, were leveled in an attempt to extinguish all memory of the former Christian presence in Turkey.

The Black Book of Communism: Crimes, Terror, Repression was published in 1997. Authored by six European academics, much of its statistical data is gleaned from recently opened archives in former Communist nations. These numbers agree regarding Marxists in the USSR as killing far more than their socialist atheist counterparts in Nazi Germany.

After World War II these numbers continued to grow as East Germany, Hungary, Poland, Yugoslavia, Czechoslovakia, and others became part of the Soviet Bloc. In 1952 the International League for the Rights of Man documented more than four hundred forced labor camps in Communist Central and Eastern Europe. Millions of people, many of whom were political prisoners only, died in these camps. One who did not was Janos Rozas. Mentioned by name in Alexander Solzhenitzyn's *The Gulag Archipelago* (1973), Rozas stated that it was only the knowledge of his innocence and his belief in God that he was able to survive the starvation, the cold, and the exhausting labor of the gulag.

Statistics in *The Black Book of Communism* arrive at over one hundred million people killed by Marxist regimes. Many reviewers of this book have questioned why the victims of Communism are not given proportional attention by the established media, education, and entertainment system. Those who decide what we see and hear have made sure everyone knows regarding Nazi Germany and its victims while saying far less about the tens of millions killed by Soviet Russia.

There is no museum in our nation's capital dedicated to the memory of the millions of victims of communism; there is no remembrance day in their honor. Neither, when the Anti-Defamation League and the Southern Poverty Law Center are invited to speak on radio, TV, and at schools and universities, are we reminded that this was the greatest of all mass murders. If mentioned at all, the atheist socialist mind-set which spawned it is not. One gets the impression that the ADL and the SPLC have more respect for atheists and socialists than the one hundred million who were their victims. *The Black Book of Communism* should be required reading in every school.

While socialist totalitarian regimes have been the greatest source of twentieth-century democide, they are not the only governments guilty of this. Many, because they were not in Europe, we are not as familiar with. The aforementioned professor, R. J. Rummel, obtained his democide statistics by studying over eight thousand reports of government-sponsored genocide, politicide, and mass murder. His total for these and the thirty-five million killed on battlefields—is a shocking 262 million.

This makes the twentieth century by far the bloodiest in human history. Since significant numbers of these people, especially in Europe, were Christians, it would be reasonable to believe that the circumstances leading to their deaths would be a type of tribulation. The same would be true of Christians persecuted under pagan Rome, the sixth beast, and papal Rome, the seventh beast. These millions, added to the previous figure, would be an incredible total.

Great Tribulation in Church History

The apostle John, in his Revelation from Jesus Christ, wrote: *I John...your brother, and companion in tribulation...* (Rev. 1:9). John, at that time (about AD 96), was *in tribulation.* Others, because of *the word of God, and for the testimony of Jesus Christ* (v. 9) were his *companion in tribulation.* In chapter 7 are 144,000 Israelites *sealed...in their foreheads* (v. 3). After this John beheld, *and, lo, a great multitude, which no man could number, of all nations, and kindreds, and people, and tongues, stood before the Lamb, clothed with white robes, and palms in their hands* (v. 9). Different and greater in number than the 144,000, these are the overcomers. And John was told: *these are they which came out of great tribulation* (v. 14). This tells us the tribulation they came out of was great, i.e., severe. Tribulation was endured by first-century Christian Israelites beginning with the stoning of Stephen in the book of Acts (7:54-60), and for some, it was, or would be *great* (i.e., greater than for others).

Tribulation continued over the centuries as the sixth, the seventh, and now the eighth, the current and last beast system, reigns over the kings of the earth. At this stage in history most of those who came out of *great tribulation* have probably been martyred, and are therefore among *the dead in Christ* and *asleep* in the grave awaiting resurrection. Stephen, the first martyr, was a tribulation saint. All among the dead in Christ, who died while persecuted for the faith, would be tribulation saints.

Of the 144,000 now dead, many were probably martyred under pagan Rome, the sixth beast, and papal Rome, the seventh beast. If a greater or lesser amount have died, or will die, under the current and last beast, the New World Order, we do not know. We do know that the twentieth century was the bloodiest in human history, a fact which tells us much of the worst is probably over. This should be comforting if one has been taught that the persecution of Christians described in Revelation is entirely yet to be.

The 144,000 According to Futurism

There is a reason why the dispensational establishment uses an application (theirs) of tribulation in which this word is preceded by "the." They do this to convey the idea of something specific to a certain time period; something which begins and ends with their futurized seventieth week. "The tribulation," according to dispensationalists, is a seven-year period commencing with "the rapture." In the case of Revelation 7:14 and others, they will attempt to convey the idea of a specific time period by referring to it as "the great tribulation."

Dr. John MacArthur of *The MacArthur Study Bible* does this to the point of including it as a heading for verses 9-17 in chapter 7. Neither, in his notes on the same, does he refer to *great tribulation* without conveniently preceding it with "the." Then, to make sure you focus on *great*, in a futuristic sense, he describes the people to whom it applies as those who did not leave in the so-called rapture.

Despite the fact that *great*, in these verses denotes, not the timing, but the severity of tribulation, MacArthur is using it to promote the future seven-year interpretation. Dispensationalists do this because of whom they identify as Israel. By adding "the" to *great*, by thus futurizing tribulation, they are able to convey the idea of a second chance for non-Christians—for the Israeli Zionists they say will comprise the 144,000.

The word *tribulation* occurs twenty-three times in Scripture, four times in the Old Testament, and nineteen times in the New. In one application only (Matt. 24:29) is it preceded with the word *the (Immediately after the tribulation of those days).* This is in reference to *the coming of the Son of man* (vv. 27, 30) that which occurs *after the tribulation of those days.* This means that the resurrection of the dead in Christ, that which occurs *at his coming* (1 Cor. 15:23), is after any and all tribulation.

Dispensationalists try to get around this by claiming that the descending of Jesus from heaven as per 1 Thessalonians 4:16 is not the second coming. They will agree that the resurrection, that the event prophesied in 1 Corinthians 15, is one and the same, but they do not like to admit that verse 23 states this will happen—*at his coming.* When reminded of their contradiction they will say that *his coming* in verse 23 is not the actual second coming, but a secret coming ("the rapture") seven years before. As explained in chapter 12 this interpretation is designed to accommodate a futurized tribulation and seventieth week, the second chance futurists need for their non-Christian "Israel."

When Israel is identified correctly we do not have to futurize the 144,000 in an attempt to reconcile with the fact they are Christian. We will not, in other words, be tempted to redefine *great* by calling *tribulation* "the tribulation." Only when Israel is identified incorrectly does one do this.

The persecution of Christians began with the stoning of Stephen in the book of Acts. *Great tribulation,* the greatest persecution, was probably under pagan Rome and papal Rome, the sixth and seventh beast systems. Tribulation, as a whole, is not over. We are no longer fed to lions nor burned at the stake, but we are, under the eighth and last beast, persecuted in other ways. Evidence for this is the millions of Christians among the 262 million people murdered by governments in the twentieth century.

As Jesus said: *In the world ye shall have tribulation: but be of good cheer; I have overcome the world* (John 16:33). Believers will see the full fruition of this at the end of the present age. Scripture references do call this, *the end of the world,* but world, in this verse, is from a Greek word meaning *age.*[28] Tribulation, in other words, will continue until the end of the present age. As for when this will be we do not know. More is said regarding how than when it will end.

Until then, tribulation, in its variety of types and degrees, will afflict Christians until divine intervention results in the removal of the wicked from government: *The Son of man shall send forth his angels, and they shall gather out of his kingdom all things that offend, and them which do iniquity* (Matt. 13:40-41). This is telling us that the wicked, that the unrighteous who currently rule in America and other Israelite nations, are going to be *cut off* (Psalm 37:34); *taken* (Matt. 24:36-44) at the end of the age. Their *iniquity,* their unrighteous laws *(things that offend),* will also be removed, i.e., erased from our statue books. There will

---

[28] *Strong's Concordance* #165, *aion,* an age (present or future).

be no more tribulation, *great* or small, when non-Christian anti-Christ people no longer rule over us. *Then shall the righteous shine forth as the sun in the kingdom of their Father* (Matt. 13:43).

Why Futurists Ignore God's Litmus Test

As a result of the futurist interpretation, millions of evangelical Christians have let their guard down. Taught to focus on *tribulation, beast,* and *anti-Christ* in a futuristic context, they do not fully recognize *the tares* and *the wicked* operating among us. Despite the fact that many in this category are openly anti-Christ, we have voted for and otherwise allowed them to attain positions of authority and influence over us.

Thanks to futurism most who accept Jesus as Messiah—*come in the flesh*—are oblivious to those who do not. God has given us a litmus test for anti-Christs (1 John 2:18; 22, 4:3; 2 John v. 7) but our clergy have little use for John's application of this word. They would rather repeat it in the context of a future dictator ("the Anti-Christ"). This allows them to divert attention from the act of rejecting/denying Jesus as

> God has given us a litmus test for anti-Christs.

Messiah (their criterion for identifying "Israel," but which John says is the mark of *an anti-Christ*). Futurists do this because they cannot reconcile their unconditional support for those perceived as Israel with those of whom John said *receive...not into your house* (2 John v. 10), and Paul, *let him be A-nath'-e-ma...* (1 Cor. 16:22).

Dispensationalists will acknowledge John's application of *anti-Christ* when writing verse-by-verse commentaries. They suggest, however, that it is limited to Christians, to false teachers among Christians. While it is true that the *many anti-Christs* (1 John 4:3) were apostate Christians, it is also true that what made them so was a denial that

Messiah *is come in the flesh.* But, was this not also a characteristic of the Judean Pharisees? And, because it was, would it not identify their modern counterparts also as anti-Christs?

Dispensationalists try to get around this by ignoring the fact that *Christ* is not a name but a title. Jesus is his name but *Christ,* the Greek equivalent of *Messiah* (Hebrew), is his title. This is why *Christ* is sometimes preceded by *the (Who is a liar but he that denieth that Jesus is the Christ? [1 John 2:22]).* To imply then that *anti-Christ* is not inclusive of all who deny that Jesus is the Christ is ludicrous.

The act of denying that Jesus is the Christ (Messiah) convicts one as *a liar* and is what John witnessed Jesus calling the Pharisees. What, then, could be more descriptive of this than modern Talmudic Phariseeism? Not only does it deny that Jesus is the Christ, but in a most blasphemous way. So the bottom line is that John did apply this word to apostate Christians, but—

> The act of denying that Jesus is the Christ (Messiah) convicts one as *a liar.*

because they were reverting to Phariseeism. *Anti-Christ,* therefore, is as much or more descriptive of today's Pharisees and their Talmud than apostate Christians.

Friends of Israel or Phariseeism?

Some who read this will be familiar with organizations such as *Friends of Israel* and other supporters of the Talmudic state. When you see an auto bumper sticker quoting Genesis 12:3 *(I will bless them that bless thee, and curse him that curseth thee...)* the driver is probably a FOI member. This person, in the vast majority of cases, will be a Christian of Anglo-Saxon, Celtic, Germanic, Scandinavian, or related European ancestry. Told, and believing, that "Israel rejected Jesus," these Christians consider today's Pharisees as Israelites and themselves, not. Thinking, then, that *thee* in Genesis 12:3

identifies those of Phariseeism, this person is advocating for a nation of the same—the self-named state of "Israel."

Do not be rude or disrespectful to these people; they sincerely believe in what they are promoting and must be tactfully approached. The best way to do this is by using the word Jew in its positive context (i.e., as on the front and rear cover of this book). The worst way is to confront them using *Jew* negatively. This is not necessary, is not consistent with its Biblical application, and—it will back-fire on you.

It cannot be emphasized to strongly that the best way to introduce Israel, correctly identified, are Biblical references in the book of Acts to those *thousands of Jews.* Use these as a stepping-stone to the general epistles (Hebrews, James, 1 Peter, etc.). Remind those who believe "Israel rejected Jesus" that this teaching cannot be reconciled with the fact that these epistles identify the first-century church as an Israelitish institution. From there go to Romans, an epistle to non-Jew Israelites. And from Romans, follow the foot-prints of these Christian Israelites from the Mediterranean area to Western Europe and America.

Do this, while emphasizing that the gospel was preached, *to the Jew first, then the Greek,* the non-Jew, Greek-speaking Israelites of the dispersion. When the first-century church is thus identified, as the thousands of Israelites who become known as Christians, FOI-type evangelicals will recognize themselves as *thee* (Genesis 12:3), as the descendants of Abraham.

"I'm Saved. What Difference Does it Make?"

Certain Christians will respond to Israel, correctly identi-fied, by saying, "What difference does it make, as long as we are saved?" This will be a person who, seeing little or no modern application in the Law of the Lord, believes in a Jesus who abrogated "the law." This person also believes they are "saved/born again" while not understanding what Jesus meant when saying, *except a man be born again he cannot see the kingdom of God* (John 3:3).

See is from a Greek word[29] meaning: To understand, i.e., or to *see.* To understand, therefore, what and where *the kingdom of God* is, one must be *born again.* Does this mean that those whose perception of the kingdom is in a go-to-heaven context do not therefore understand it and are not therefore born again? Does this explain why so many Christians do not understand *the gospel of the kingdom,* the message preached by Jesus and the New Testament writers? This seems to be the case.

Those who perceive *the kingdom of God* as other than an earth-based Christian theocracy see little or no value in the Law of the Lord. After all, they are going to be floating around up in heaven, are they not? And why would God's laws statutes and judgments be needed up there? To *see,* then, *the kingdom of God* from a go-to-heaven perspective is the equivalent of not seeing (i.e., understanding) the kingdom of God. This is very serious.

The New Testament tells us it is *Israelites: to whom pertaineth...the law.* Most evangelicals, regarding this law, are as sheep without a shepherd. The sermons and other instruction they receive say much about grace, but very little regarding the statutes and judgments in the Law of the Lord. They know that *thou shalt not kill* prohibits axe murdering, that *thou shalt not steal* prohibits shoplifting, and that *thou shalt not bear false witness* prohibits lying about someone, but they are unaware that each of the Ten Commandments is but a brief summary of the Law of the Lord in a specific area.

---

[29] *Eido,* Strong's #1492, to see, figuratively only, be aware of, perceive, understand.

This writer has met "born again," evangelical Christians who leave church on Sunday to patronize buffet restaurants at gambling casinos. Most evangelicals know better than this, but are, in other areas, transgressing the Law of the Lord. Usury, the using of money to multiply itself, is one of these. Scripture tells us to be content with *food and raiment,* that they who *will be rich fall into a temptation and a snare* because *the love of money is the root of all evil: which while some coveted after, they have erred from the faith* (1 Tim. 6:8-10). And we claim to believe this, even as we covet money, as most of us err from the faith by putting it out to usury.

Why, when those who *nameth the name of Christ* are told to *depart from iniquity* (2 Tim. 2:19) do we reap where we did not sow (Luke 19:22-23) by putting money out to usury? Why, when Jesus warned regarding those who heareth his words on this and other subjects *and doeth them not* (Matt. 7:26), do we fall for the permissiveness of antinomian teaching? Are we like the *foolish man, which built his house upon the sand?*

Why Few Are Saved and Many Lost

In his prelude to the Sermon on the Mount Jesus said, *think not that I am come to destroy the law.* Then, while defining righteousness in the context of this law (The Law of the Lord) he warned his audience: *except your righteousness shall exceed the righteousness of the scribes and Pharisees, ye shall in no case enter in to the kingdom of heaven.* This tells us that our righteousness, that our obedience to the Law of the Lord, must exceed that of the clergy in his day. But what, regarding this law, do the clergy in our day tell us? Little if at all, and when they do address the subject it is probably to imply that it is either, not for us, or is somehow irrelevant in a modern society.

This, because it cannot be reconciled with the teachings of Jesus, explains the connection between his prophetic statement regarding *iniquity*/lawlessness (Matt. 7:21-23) and the *mark of the beast* in the book of Revelation. We should not, therefore, limit this to a RFID or literal mark (tattoo, etc.) in some future-only period. Emphasis, rather, should be given to *iniquity* (i.e., lawlessness), that which is opposite *the commandments of God.*

While it is possible that those who currently *reigneth over the kings of the earth* (Rev. 17:18) could, eventually, mandate a RFID or literal mark of some kind, it, if implemented, would not have to be *the mark,* i.e., it would not have to be a literal 666 in one's right hand or forehead. The number 666 is symbolic—symbolic of an antinomian mind-set. We should not, therefore, perceive *the mark of the beast* as a literal tattoo; it should be understood in the context of *iniquity* (Matt. 7:23, i.e., lawlessness) and a worldview based upon it.

How to Avoid Those Awful Words of Jesus

Chapter 14 of Revelation opens with *a Lamb,* with Jesus standing on *the mount Zion.* With him are the 144,000, those described in chapter 7 as *sealed...in their foreheads* and now the same, but stated as *having his Father's name written in their foreheads. Mount Zion,* in the context of Revelation, is prophetic. Just as there is a prophetic *new Jerusalem,* that which descends *out of heaven from God* (Rev. 21:2, 10), so is there a prophetic Zion. Each denotes a place of governmental authority, a cleansed kingdom of God. The administrators in this kingdom would be the 144,000. Also present in this Christian theocracy, but with, apparently, a lesser role, are the *great multitude* in chapter 7, again described as from *every nation, and kindred, and tongue, and people* (14:6). It is therefore the 144,000 and those of this greater number who, as described in the gospels and epistles, *inherit the kingdom of God.* What separates them from those who received the mark of the beast is revealed in the following:

Here is the patience of the saints: here are they that
keep the commandments of God, and the faith of Jesus.
Revelation 14:12 (emphasis mine)

Here is another reminder, a double witness, to the fact that
it is the keeping of *the commandments of God* which is also
the faith of Jesus, and—which sets one apart from those who
receive the mark of the beast, the lawless beast system called
Mystery, Babylon the Great. We are told: *Come out of her, my
people, that ye be not partakers of her sins.* God's Israel covenant people *(my people)* are to come out of, to not partake
in this beast system, in this government-sanctioned lawlessness. Christians who do not heed this warning, who ignore
John's reminder that *sin is the transgression of the law,* will
hear those awful words: *I never knew you: depart from me,
ye that work iniquity.*

This and other reasons are why we should not assume,
because we are Christian—that we are not Israelites—
that we are not those whose responsibility it is to obey
the Law of the Lord.

The author in his backyard.

ABOUT THE AUTHOR

Jaye Torgerson, a longtime student of Scripture and Christian history, has authored numerous related and nonrelated articles. In the mid-1980s he became aware of the gospel of the kingdom, the message preached by Jesus and the New Testament writers. Over the years this key to understanding led to an unlocking of additional truths and a desire to share them with others in a book.

The author grew up and currently resides in rural Eau Claire, Wisconsin. Retired, he and his wife have three grown children, all raised on the wooded hideaway they call West Creek Acres. Some of his hobbies are hunting and fishing, gardening, bird-watching, following national and world affairs, and meeting with the writer's guild of which he is a member. For a brief answer to questions and comments regarding the subject matter in this book, e-mail Jaye at *info@jewandnonjewisraelites.com.*

**Jew and Non-Jew Israelites
is available online at**

Amazon.com and BarnesandNoble.com

Wholesale price available for orders of ten and more at

www.jewandnonjewisraelites.com

INDEX

Hebrew University, 117
heirs according to the promise,
    38
Henry, Matthew, 101
Hertz, Rabbi Joseph, 114
historic Christianity, 32
history's bloodiest century,
    178
Hitler, Adolph, 178
Hobby Lobby, 160
Hollywood, 136
Holocaust, 178
Howse, Brannon, 77, 78
Hungary, 180

I

idea of second chance, 183
incognito, 176
income tax, 168
in context, 148
India and China, 123
indigenous people, 125
I never knew you, 142
inherit the kingdom, 77
iniquity, 67
In My Father's House, 95
Inquisition, 126, 163
invisible government, 167
Iraq, 171
Ironsides, Harry, 88
IRS (Internal Revenue Service),
    168
Isaac and Rebekah, 122
Israel carried away, 9
Israelites, 48
Israelites marrying Israelites,
    122
Israelitish institution, 130
Israeli Zionists, 183
Israel mine elect, 42

J

Jackson, Andrew, 168, 174
Jacob, 49, 90
James, 41
Jamieson, 101
Jenkins, Jerry, 108
Jennings, Charles, 164
Jeremiah's prophecy, 39
Jerusalem Countdown, 108
Jesus—a real Jew, 25
Jesus, the real, 62
Jew, is a, 19
Jewish DNA, 117
Jewish Voice Ministries, 118
Jewish Voice TV program, 118
Jew, not a, 19
Jews accepting Jesus, 37
Jews, convinced the, 31
Jews, real, 30
Job, 71
Joel's prophecy, 55
Johns Hopkins School of Public
    Health, 117
John the Baptist, 34
Jonah, 81
Joseph of Arimathaea, 25
Judah, 9
Judahites to Judeans, 13
Judas Iscariot, 14
Judean Pharisees, 15
Judeo-Christian eschatology,
    107
Judith the Hittite, 122
Jutes, 123

K

Kaganovich, Lazar, 177
KGB, 177
Khazarian, 117
Khazar tribes, 113

New Covenant, 56, 124
Newton, Sir Isaac, 141
New World, 126
New World Order, 136, 164
New York, 173
New York Times, 177
Nicholas II, 173
non-Christian people, 65
non-Israelitish, 46
non-Israelitish "Jews", 118
non-Jew Diaspora Israelites,
   52, 57
non-Jew Israelites, 42, 43, 59
non-Messianic Jews, 22
no respecter of, 51
no second chance, 103, 165
not by coincidence, 123
no third time, 151
not in heaven, 96
not of Judah, 116
number 666, not a tattoo, 157,
   190

O

Obama, Barack, 171
Old Hickory, 174
olive trees, 55
Oppenheim, Ariella, 117
opposite is true, 127
oracles of God, 29, 125
other families of the earth, 64
other sheep, 60
Other sheep, 10
Ottoman Empire, 179

P

pagan concept, 63
Pentecost, 55
People's Republic of China, 178
persecuted us, 16

Peter, 55
Peter, First Epistle of, 42
Peter's vision, 43
Pharisees, today's, 100, 126
Pitts, F. E., 128
pluralism, 160
Poland, 180
Pollock, Nathan M., 116
Ponzi scheme, 169
pornography, 152
postmillennial, 91
Pot, Pol, 178
premillennial, 91
professing Jews only, 24
professing-only Jews, 22
promises, 54
proselytes, 115
Protestant Reformers, 40, 87
purgatory, 63, 82
Puritans, 123

R

raise the dead, 72
rapture, 87, 88, 89, 91
real Jew, 20
Rebekah, 125
reconciled, 56
Redeemer of Israel, 33
red heifer, 102
reincarnation, 63
remnant, 9
remnant of Judahites, 41
repentance, 66
Replacement Theology, 47
resurrection, 72
resurrection, first, 87, 92, 106
returns, 9
RFID (Radio-Frequency
   IDentification), 157, 163,
   190

www.ingramcontent.com/pod-product-compliance
Lightning Source LLC
La Vergne TN
LVHW051511080426
835509LV00017B/2031